—Elizabeth N

Precious Treasure
The Story of PAtriUk

EMMAUS
ROAD
PUBLISHING
Steubenville, Ohio
A Division of Catholics United for the Faith

With a Foreword by Kimberly Hahn

Emmaus Road Publishing
827 North Fourth Street
Steubenville, Ohio 43952

Library of Congress Control Number: 2002104194
ISBN 1-931018-13-8

Cover photography by
Stacy Bryant

Cover design and layout by
Beth Hart

Precious Treasure

To my husband, Mark, and our dear children,
Sean, Laura, Patrick, Brendan, Megan, Michael, Kathryn,
Bridget, Emily, and Connor, who have worked overtime
helping this poor mother of theirs on the path to holiness.
I am eternally grateful for the beautiful blessing
each one of you is in my life.

*"Whoever receives one such child
in my name receives me."*

—Matthew 18:5

Contents

— *Contents* —

— Contents —

Foreword

$\mathscr{I}$ have always been told that God had a marvelous plan for my life. Once I united my life to Scott Hahn's in holy matrimony, I hoped that plan would involve a half dozen little ones, and it has. We are living out this marvelous plan, with all of its joys and sorrows, through sickness and health, in plenty and in want—materially, emotionally, and spiritually. It is a marvelous life together, though not without conflicts, difficulties, and sufferings. In fact, it is marvelous because of what God is doing in and through us in the midst of challenges.

The Hahn family is not different from the Matthews family or yours. Each day is a new day to embrace the fullness of the vocation of marriage and family life. Though the struggles that Beth shares are particular to her family, with one child having severe autism, you will notice a number of points of similarity, as did I, between her reflections on parenting and your own experience.

Our children teach us every day about our relationship with our heavenly Father, both through their childlikeness and their childishness. We see their pure joy over the simplest things and realize how much more thankful to God we need to be for His many blessings in our lives. We watch their simple trust in us and in God, and we recognize our need to place our lives more fully in our Father's hands. We also see our own willfulness reflected in their childish choices to ignore our commands. And like our children, our own lack of understanding how, or why, to obey can lead to frustration and anger in them and in us.

Parenting is a daunting task. Some of our children are so much like us—we understand them better than our other children—but in struggling with the shortcomings and character flaws that we see reflected in them, we struggle with ourselves. Some of our children are very different from us in personality, giftedness, or temperament, and we struggle to understand them as they struggle to understand us. There are times when conflicts can be resolved by a quick trip to the confessional and an apology; other times, we need the input that only professionals can bring.

Beth Matthews gives us a glimpse into the ongoing challenges she and her husband face because of their child's special needs. As she identifies those challenges and reflects on what she has learned in her own relationship with the Lord, I see ways I struggle with similar challenges in my family:

- Where is God when our children are hurting?
- How do I face my own limitations in solving a problem?
- How do I face those limitations with my spouse, who also feels limited?
- How do I keep on target with the priorities of our family's life in the midst of a particular challenge?
- How can I see the hand of the God in the ordinary today?
- How does God want me to change, rather than how do I get God to change someone or something?

The particular children Our Lord has given us are a unique part of our path towards sanctity. Whether or not we know someone who is more patient, loving, or kind than we are, God has chosen us for the task of parenting these boys or girls, and we are the right parents for them. That being said, don't all of us have a long way to go to be perfect parents or perfect children? So how do we get from here to there?

We follow the path of sanctity by embracing the joys and the sufferings that accompany each of us through the others.

There are many little humiliations along the way as we fail at our task of parenting. We have a saying in our family that we picked up from a wonderful priest, Father Joe. Since the core sin we battle is pride, whatever takes a whack at pride helps us move along in the right direction. So, if (or rather, when) we fail our children, we embrace that humiliation and ask their forgiveness. Just taking a whack at pride makes us better parents—and it shows our children how to grow in holiness, too.

Today, many good people seem to lack confidence in themselves as parents. Beth Matthews shares both her strengths and her weaknesses in such a way that you will be drawn into a glimpse of yourself. You will laugh with her and cry with her. And in the midst of it all, you will appreciate more deeply than before your own family and the ways in which the Lord is using your loved ones to draw your heart closer to Him.

KIMBERLY HAHN

A Letter to Readers
from a Daddy's Heart

Count it all joy, my brethren,
when you meet various trials.
—James 1:2

About eleven years ago, God sent my family on a strange but wonderful journey. In 1991, our third child, Patrick, was diagnosed with autism, and so our odyssey began. Regardless of the medication, diet, treatment, or teacher, Patrick has improved little. I'll admit it has been frustrating at times, but my wife, Beth, and I believe that God has a special plan for Patrick and us. The journey has been difficult because each road we've traveled has reached a dead end. Although we've had no success in finding a cure, we believe that God has asked us to travel each of these roads for some reason. We may not know what the reason is, now or ever, but He has permitted each step of our journey to occur.

I suspect God has allowed Patrick's condition to continue because He still has a lot to teach us. I know I'm still trying to learn from each step along the way. In many ways, this odyssey has been wonderful because of the support of so many of God's people. We have been shown the Body of Christ in ways that I could never have anticipated or imagined. People have been so very good to us and to Patrick, and for this I'll be forever grateful.

I will always remember the day we received the diagnosis of autism. I remember it most because I knew so little about autism then. In 1991, it was still a relatively rare condition, or so I believed. The therapist from Indiana University who diagnosed Patrick immediately began to offer information about how to join family support groups. I knew she was trying to help, but I didn't feel a need to join a support group. Since then, however, I've realized that family support groups can be wonderful avenues for relaying information, for learning more about disabilities, and for helping one another with the difficulties of raising special children. Thank God we were blessed already with so much support from the people at our parish, Our Lady of Mount Carmel in Carmel, Indiana, and our families have been with us throughout. I realize it is very difficult for some parents to accept that their child is different or handicapped in some way, but it has never been hard for me. Through God's grace, He allowed me to accept Patrick and his condition, just as He has allowed me to accept our other nine children and their unique qualities. I simply believed God had a very special plan for Patrick, and I knew somehow I would participate in that plan.

As I said, I knew very little about autism then. I don't know nearly enough now, but I can explain some of its characteristics. Broadly defined, it is a social and communicative disorder. It is often referred to as a spectrum disorder, because its symptoms may occur in any combination with varying degrees of severity. Some autistic people are able to function rather normally in society; others live in their own little worlds. Today, autism is one of the most common developmental disabilities, affecting as many as one in two hundred children. Some believe it is reaching epidemic proportions. There is no cure for autism, though many autistic people have been aided through medication, diet, and education.

Patrick's autism manifested itself around the age of two; he had developed normally for the first year or so of his life. We lived in southern California then, and I remember him standing in his crib looking out the window of our apartment at cars and saying, "Car, car," at about twelve months. Patrick used a few other words, but soon he lost them. He acted as if he couldn't hear, and he wouldn't follow even simple directions.

We became more aware of a problem because he wasn't developing as our two older children, Sean and Laura, had. Both of them had been early talkers. They were imaginative and playful. Patrick was aloof, even distant. He loved rough-housing and swinging but was reluctant to join in any games. He was content to watch movies or entertain himself with little figurines. People often commented that he was "such a good baby."

Unlike many autistic children, Patrick has always been very loving towards my wife and me. He would sit on our laps and loved being hugged. He still does. Patrick was clearly not interested in playing with other children, however, and the most we could ever hope for was the occasional parallel play with one of his brothers or sisters. Despite his loving attitude, he has always preferred to be alone. Patrick can spend hours in the yard going from a swing set to a trampoline and back again. Then again, he may come to one of us, lift up his shirt, and say, "Tickle, tickle." ("Tickle" is one of the few words Patrick has ever said.)

When Patrick was about two and a half, Beth was part of a Bible study at Our Lady of Mount Carmel. She listened as a woman prayed for her autistic son, Mikey. Later, she asked the woman about her son. In describing Mikey's actions and behavior, she could have been describing Patrick as well. For the first time, we had a name to attach to what was going on with our little boy. We knew there was some problem, but we really didn't know what. We had suspected that Patrick couldn't hear, but tests proved he could. We had wondered if there was a mental deficiency. Whatever the case, we needed a diagnosis to qualify for early intervention services. Reluctantly, the therapist gave us the diagnosis we suspected.

We have traveled around the country to hospitals, schools, and clinics over the past eleven years in search of help. We have researched autism, consulted doctors and therapists, tried medications, placed Patrick in a developmental preschool and then in special education programs, and changed his diet more than a few times.

Over the next several years, I had to become a very creative father to keep up with Patrick. I had to learn to live with less sleep and expect the unexpected. Beth has written of many of his adventures in the pages of this book, but I have many memories that are not shared here. I have come home to find Patrick on the roof of our two-story house, have watched as he taught himself to swim, have learned to communicate through signs and gestures, and have worried that he would hurt himself by falling off the top of our play gym. In the years since Patrick's birth, we have had seven more children: Brendan, Megan, Michael, Kate, Bridget, Emily, and Connor. The challenges of a large family are considerable. Add to that a mentally handicapped child who appears normal to outsiders at first glance, and you have a recipe for some interesting situations.

One very negative side of autism that can surface at any time but most often occurs at puberty is aggression. Sometimes this manifests itself in self-mutilation as well. This aggression appeared in Patrick at around the age of nine and a half, and by the age of ten and a half, it was out of control. Medication wasn't helping. Patrick had always been very gentle and passive, and he never hurt anyone. Suddenly, he started to strike at me, Beth, or one of the other children. His aggression usually was triggered when someone told him no to something he wanted and couldn't have. He may have wanted food that wasn't on his diet or a toy that someone else had.

At times, Patrick would strike others for no reason. When he began to hit or kick his smaller brothers or sisters, we knew we had to get help for both him and his siblings. Our strongest desire has always been to provide for Patrick in our home. If Patrick were going to continue to live at home, we would have to take drastic measures to change his behavior. Because of this, we placed Patrick at Silvercrest Children's Developmental Center, a residential school about two hours from our home. It is located in a former tuberculosis hospital on top of a hill that overlooks Louisville, Kentucky, and the Ohio River. The school provides short-term placement for children with developmental disabilities or behavioral problems. At his admission conference, the staff recommended a one-year placement.

We had been hoping for the minimum placement of two months, but Patrick needed much more help. Beth and I have never done anything more difficult in our lives than agree to send Patrick away to school. The Tuesday after Thanksgiving, 1999, Patrick moved to Silvercrest.

Beth wrote many letters to Patrick while he was away. Because Patrick cannot read, the letters were never sent. This book contains the letters she wrote, along with stories of the tremendous blessing Patrick is for our family. Beth wrote about moments of prayer and the insight with which God has blessed her to help her through the struggles. Along with those moments are many memories of pain and struggle, joy and laughter, heartache and tears. She wrote to share Patrick, one of our precious treasures.

I will be eternally grateful to all of the family, friends, and even strangers who have interceded on behalf of one special little boy. Much of what they have done is described in the pages of this book. Some is known to God alone. Suffice it to say, I have learned more about myself and my faith because of Patrick and this journey. Through it all, Patrick has remained our little miracle from God. He has brought me closer to God than I could ever have imagined. I hope this book brings you, the reader, closer to Him, too. May God bless you abundantly.

MARK MATTHEWS

Introduction

_L_ike my son Patrick, I was the third child in a large family. My parents, Donald and Kathleen Gibbons, were actually quite normal in having such a large family. In fact, many of my friends came from families larger than mine. Our neighborhood on the north side of Indianapolis was a sea of children. I can't imagine growing up in a more wonderful environment. It was obvious to me as a child that life was a special gift from God, something never to be rejected. I could see this in the way the beautiful people of our parish, Saint Joan of Arc, celebrated each birth and mourned each death.

Today, it is not easy to move unnoticed around town with ten children, so I rarely try. When I do try, I am often asked many interesting questions. Sometimes I wonder if people really want to know the answers. One very common comment is, "How do you keep track of all of them? You must have to stop and count all the time." I answer, "I don't have to count them, because everyone else does it for me." I hear the whispering comments like, "Nine. Nine children. Did you count nine?" and "Yes, I'm sure I counted nine." I don't mind. Now that Connor has been born, I'll soon hear the sweet sounds of "Ten. Yes, I'm sure I counted ten."

Once as I was shopping at the grocery store, just before my ninth child, Emily, was born, I watched as a woman came running from a few aisles over to see "the woman who has nine children." It all started when someone stocking shelves asked if I was having my first child. When I told her I had eight children at home, she yelled to another employee that I was having my ninth, and suddenly I was on display.

I am no longer surprised at what people say. The worst comment from my perspective was listening to a checkout clerk describe the different forms of contraception she's used with each of her husbands. I could only pray for her and thank God my older children were not with me. One of the funniest comments is, "Obviously, you don't work." In response to that comment, I just smile and say, "No, I play all day."

The list of comments goes on and on, but the ones that pull at my heart the most claim that children are a burden to be endured and the cause of a great deal of trouble. Recently, I watched a very "together," fashionable saleswoman fall apart when she heard I had ten children. She blurted out, "Oh, you poor thing." Then she caught herself and turned away. I think she could see on my face what was in my heart, and she had nothing more to say.

One of the most common comments I hear, and one of the most painful, is, "I don't know how you do it. I have two, and that's it for me. They are driving me crazy." At that moment, I can actually feel a pain in my heart. My heart aches for the mother and father. I want to sit down with them and take them step-by-step through the Bible, discuss their lives and the lives of their children, and show them that children are always and only a blessing. I want to speak with them about a self-centered life—one seen in magazines and movies—that will lead only to emptiness, sorrow, unhappiness, and possibly even death of the soul, and I want to tell them how God uses His precious little ones to save us from such emptiness. Pope John Paul II says, "Life has meaning to the extent it becomes a free gift for others."[1]

---

[1] Pope John Paul II, *Crossing the Threshold of Hope* (New York: Knopf, 1994), 121.

I often wonder how we have gotten to the point where we see the very beautiful blessing of children as the cause of so much pain. Many of us want to be holy, but few of us want the pain that accompanies holiness. Dying to self is painful, but we experience more pain when we won't let go. There has to be someone else responsible for pain other than ourselves, and that someone is often a child. In essence, our world has been blinded to the blessing of children.

So many people are praying for Patrick. One night, as we were driving home in the van with the children praying the Rosary, it came to me that a certain priest, Father Michael Scanlan, chancellor of Franciscan University of Steubenville, was supposed to pray over Patrick. We called someone who knew the priest. Within hours, this acquaintance of Father Scanlan called me back and we talked. He called a friend of his who then arranged for us to meet not with Father Scanlan, but with a very holy woman from Trinidad named Babsie Bleasdell, who many say has the gift of healing. The next day, she was to be at a conference within a few hours' drive of our home. Some friends of ours, the Clinkenbeards, did not hesitate to spend their Saturday watching all our other children. When Babsie prayed over Patrick, the peace and love that filled the room was tremendous. She said, "Patrick will talk, but it will be only in God's time. For right now, He is busy making saints."

I'm not sure what happened that day, but I do know that there was an outpouring of God's grace that touched the lives of all of us. Many good and holy people have prayed over Patrick and continue to pray for him. It was not the first or the last time that many people came forward to make it possible for us to travel with Patrick wherever God was leading.

Why God has placed us on this seemingly endless search for a cure, we do not know. The questions are endless. What we try to ask in each situation is how our search has brought us closer to God. We do not know why He has led us to so many possible cures, only to see little or no improvement in Patrick's condition. In some instances, Patrick has even become worse. We do know that God could cure him in the twinkling of an eye according to His plan. God's plan is awesome, of that we can be sure.

And so, I have written this book from my heart about one of my precious treasures, Patrick. I wrote this book to open the eyes of those who do not recognize the priceless gift of children in their lives, and to encourage those who do recognize the worth of children. I especially would like to appeal to those who have special-needs children. Patrick's autism has been a most incredible gift for us. It is not what we would have chosen. In many ways, however, God has used Patrick's special needs to draw our family closer to Him.

CHAPTER ONE

My Escalator to Heaven

November 30, 1999

My dear Patrick,

Today Mommy and Daddy did the hardest thing we've ever done in our lives. I know you don't understand. We could see the confusion in your eyes as you cried and pulled on Daddy's hand trying to go with us. You must have wondered, "Why are they leaving me here? What is happening?" The tears in your eyes were enough to let us know you wanted to go home with us. I wanted so much to grab you and run to the car, but I knew it would only hurt you more, and your pain was already stabbing my heart.

I pray your new room gives you some comfort. Your godparents, Aunt Mary and Uncle Gary, decorated your room for you with some of your favorite movie themes, hoping it would make you happy. They love you so much, Patrick. Grandma Gibbons wanted you to have something special to hold, so she bought you the big teddy bear on your bed. It is hard for her to be so far away in San Diego. I have a small teddy bear just like yours that I keep on the cabinet in the dining room by your picture. Even though it does not ease the pain, it reminds me that soon I will again have you in my arms.

This pain I'm feeling is one I felt ten and a half years ago, just a few days after you were born. You were taken to the intensive care unit for babies because you had a little fever, and your breathing was very fast. The doctors didn't know what was wrong, and they had you hooked up to many monitors. It was so hard to leave you there, but I had to go home for a short while to see Sean and Laura. They were still so small when you were born, and they missed their mommy. I left the hospital and walked out into the bright April sunshine; it was an unusually warm day. Every step that took me farther from you hurt. I wanted so much to run into the hospital and grab and hold you.

I needed to make sure nothing would happen to you while I was away. I asked God to send His angels to be with you, to comfort and to protect you. I'm once again asking Him to send the angels because I don't know if you are cold, hungry, or frightened. I lie awake here wondering and crying. Daddy and I have both been crying since we walked away from you, but we have found a great deal of strength in holding each other and praying for you. Patrick, you are such a precious little treasure to us. We miss you. God bless you, my little one.

I love you,
Mommy

[M]ay . . . the eyes of your hearts [be] enlightened, that you may know what is the hope to which he has called you, what are the riches of his glorious inheritance in the saints.

—Ephesians 1:17-19

Many have heard of a stairway to heaven, but I'm sure few have heard of an escalator to heaven. My escalator came in the form of a beautiful child named Patrick. He has been a channel of much grace for me and my family. He has a way of helping me to embrace and love the pain and suffering that come with denial of my will and total submission to the will of God. God is using a precious child to carry me to heaven.

Thoughts of an escalator to heaven take me back long ago, to a place in Peru. I was spending a month there between my junior and senior years of high school helping my uncle, Father John Tasto, with his missionary work in the Andes Mountains.

I stayed with a group of Benedictine sisters in the village of Santo Domingo, in a little convent nestled in the mountains. Santo Domingo was founded by colonists from Spain who came over the Andes to settle several hundred years ago. The people live in small adobe huts and travel by foot on dirt roads to their sugarcane fields and cornfields. The farmers plant the corn right up the side of the mountain. The Catholic parish is in the town square in the center of the village. The people have a deep, beautiful, but simple faith.

One day after closing her clinic, where she cared for many sick and injured people each day, Sister Romaine asked me if I would like to accompany her on a walk to care for an elderly lady. Sister informed me that the walk would be a little over an hour long, and even though an hour seemed an awfully long time to walk to give just one treatment to one lady, I agreed to go along. We walked on the dirt road for a short while on that warm, sunny day, and then I noticed an opening in the rocks along the side of the road. Sister stopped at the opening, and I could not believe we actually were going to climb up those rocks. The huge boulders and smaller rocks formed a path straight up the mountain. I hoped that somewhere beyond where I could see would be a smooth, flat road. I lost that hope when Sister told me that we would be climbing the rocks all the way up. My jaw dropped to the ground. For me, a city girl from Indianapolis, a walk was something you did for fun on a smooth, perfectly flat sidewalk, or at the mall. This was far more than I was prepared for, and I wasn't sure I could make it. If Sister was going to climb, however, I decided I would go along with her.

We paused before we began, and I turned to Sister and said, "It looks like a stairway of rocks. Now if we could only push a button and get these rocks to move and turn into an escalator . . ." We laughed and began our climb. Little did I know the impact that statement would have on my life. As we walked, my lungs began to ache because the air was thin. As I looked at Sister, she smiled. I knew she had bad knees and must be in pain, but she showed no signs of distress other than stopping once in a while to rub her knees. While I watched her make that climb that day, I knew that she possessed something very beautiful. Something had indeed turned her mountain of rocks into an escalator. When we arrived at the little adobe home of the old woman, it became clear to me that what Sister possessed was a beautiful ability to see Christ in this poor, helpless woman. As she climbed, she knew she was climbing to see Jesus. I thought to myself, "Is it possible to embrace such pain?"

In my heart, I asked God to give me an escalator, but I would never have dreamed that He would bless me with one in the form of a special little boy. I did not know that God would allow my beautiful little baby to be afflicted with the cold and painful disorder of autism.

Many years after my first climb up the escalator with Sister, I drove down the highway with the words of the specialist running through my mind over and over again: "Your son is autistic." Even though we had expected the diagnosis for months, the confirmation was piercing. The tears filled my eyes and then flowed down my cheeks. I could feel a child within me, little Megan, our fifth child, as she moved about. Once again, I thought, "God has blessed our family with new life. What would this new life hold for her with an autistic brother?" I had many thoughts running through my head, but I couldn't contain the overwhelming feelings of peace and joy in my heart. I knew that these feelings were not of my own doing but were from the grace that I had asked from God over and over again in my life.

As a nursing student, I prayed for God's grace on many nights after hours of study, before every test, and after Communion at daily Mass. I knew I would never make it through nursing school on my own, and the fear of failing was more than I could handle. A complete peace and joy came over me each time I placed my will into the gentle hands of my heavenly Father. He took away my desire for a degree in nursing and left me with a desire only to do His will, however He asked. My prayer was the beautiful prayer of Saint Ignatius of Loyola:

Take, Lord, receive all my liberty,
my memory, my understanding,
and my entire will,
all that I have and possess.
You have given all to me,
To you, O Lord, I return it.
All is yours; dispose of it wholly according to your will.
Give me only your love and your grace,
for this is enough for me.

A few years later, after my first child, Sean, was born, I prayed the prayer again as I sat in a cold hospital room with Mark beside me. The woman in the bed next to me had a beautiful baby in her arms. My arms were empty. At that time the only memory I had of my son was of his being rushed off to the intensive care unit. I didn't even get a chance to touch him. The doctors explained that he had severe meconium aspiration syndrome. Meconium, a black, tarry substance, is a baby's first stool. Because of stress during labor, Sean's stool was released into the amniotic fluid and had filled his lungs. At birth the doctors wouldn't let him cry for fear he would inhale more meconium. Within seconds he was whisked away to the special-care nursery.

He was placed on a respirator, was given antibiotics, and received respiratory therapy. Only time would tell if he would survive. If he did, the list of possible complications was frightening. The chaplain even suggested that we have Sean baptized. Numb, Mark and I prayed together, thanking God for the nine months we had had with Sean. We asked Him for the grace to see each and every moment with Sean as a precious gift from Him. Much as Mary and Joseph presented Jesus in the Temple, we gave Sean back to God. Then God intervened and performed miracles. As quickly as a doctor would explain a potential complication to us, another doctor would come and say that we had passed that hurdle. After a week of sleepless nights, many treatments, and much prayer, we took home our perfectly healthy baby boy. Today he is preparing to study for the priesthood.

As I drove down the highway with Patrick beside me, once again I prayed the prayer of Saint Ignatius of Loyola and asked for the grace to cherish every moment with Patrick, just the way he is. The tears rolled down my face. I thought, "He may never play ball, or say 'Mommy,' but he will always be a special child of God." And then it came to me: God had blessed me with an escalator to heaven, just what I had prayed for over ten years before. God knew my weakness. He knew I needed much more than a stairway, so He gave me the hand of my beautiful son and asked me to ride. Sometimes the escalator stops; sometimes it goes in reverse; but always it points towards heaven.

I have a treasure of my own of gold and silver,
and because of my devotion to the house of my God
I give it to the house of my God.

—1 Chronicles 29:3

CHAPTER TWO

Be Still

December 8, 1999

My dear Patrick,

We miss you so much. Everything in the house is different without you here to give it your own special touch. I know how much you like being around things that you know, things that are familiar to you. You do not know these people who are taking care of you and teaching you, but God does. In fact, He has it all planned out very well.

Many years ago, you were being moved to a new school closer to home. As much as you liked riding on the bus, I was happy that you wouldn't have to ride quite as long. My greatest concern was that the school year was about to begin, and they did not have a teacher for your class. Many people encouraged us to consider sending you to a private school about a half hour from our home where you would have a wonderful teacher named Rita Popp, who was known for her work with autistic children. We knew we could not send you there for two main reasons. First, the cost was more than we could afford, and second, the transportation was not provided. With a house full of little ones, I did not know how I could get you back and forth to school.

Daddy and I knew that God did not want us to send you there. We knew that we had to trust in God, and He would provide the teacher. A few weeks before school started, I received a phone call from the woman who was to be your new teacher. I almost dropped the phone when she said her name was Rita Popp. Yes, God brought your special teacher to you. I know how much you love her and all the teachers and therapists who have helped you so much.

Patrick, I know your new teacher is very special. I could not have left you in her care if I did not see in her eyes a love for special children like you. You can go to her to be held, or to receive a kiss when you are hurt. She will hold you and wipe away your tears. I wonder if the flow of tears will ever stop. I love you so much. God bless you, my little one.

I love you,
Mommy

Do all things without grumbling or questioning, that you may be blameless and innocent, children of God.

—*Philippians 2:14*

Often, people have called me stubborn or strong willed. When I used to get an idea of how something ought to be done, it was nearly impossible to convince me otherwise. I could become very frustrated when things didn't go the way I thought was best. I would work full speed ahead to accomplish what I thought needed to be done, or get what I thought I needed. Sometimes I attempted these things with unrealistic expectations for myself and others. My stubbornness is something I do recognize in myself, so I will be the first to admit it. I knew in my mind that I wanted only God's will, but in my heart I was really thinking, "Your will be done, Lord, as long as it's my will." However, I never really thought anything of it until I changed a diaper. This was not just any diaper, though. I was third in a family of nine children, so there were always diapers to be changed. Also, I spent many years baby-sitting, so the art of changing diapers was one I thought I had mastered.

God opened my eyes to my strong-willed tendencies when I changed one particular diaper. It wasn't a pretty sight, but then, neither was my strong will. Patrick was a toddler on the go with a dirty diaper, and to top it all off, he had a diaper rash. Patrick and I struggled that day, for he had one thing in mind and one thing only, and that was food. He was ready to fight against the diaper change with everything he had, and so I experienced an awakening to just what damage a misguided strong will can do.

Patrick was hungry. I knew he was hungry because, for one thing, he was always hungry, and for another, when I caught him climbing to reach the food cabinet for some crackers, I noticed the incriminating smell. I could see it had leaked out the side of his pants, and I knew I had to act quickly or there would be a greater price to pay.

Patrick had other plans. He had stacked up chairs and climbed to the top of the cabinets. At this point, he clearly had no intention of stopping his quest for food. Patrick at nearly three could not speak, so I couldn't talk to him about different options. I quickly lifted him off the chairs, and holding him firmly, I rushed off for the inevitable.

I held him down and began to cut away the black electrical tape we used to hold his diaper on. Strange as it may sound, electrical tape was the only way we could find to keep him from taking his diaper off. We had little rolls of it stashed all over the house. A somewhat difficult procedure became all the more difficult when he began to kick and pull away. At this point, there was no turning back. His bottom was bright red, and since his skin was so sensitive, I knew he was in a lot of pain. I also knew that food was very comforting to Patrick, and I could only imagine that he was thinking, "I am hurting, and if I could only get some food, I would feel better." He was determined to fight me with every ounce of energy he had.

Through all this, I just kept thinking to myself, "If you would only lie still and let me change your diaper, I could have given you the food long ago. The pain would be gone, and you could be eating those crackers you want so badly." By this time, the mess had spread, and the only hope of ever cleaning Patrick was a bath. Patrick loves a bath when he wants it, but he did not want one then. So the struggle continued. I was in tears, not over the mess, but over the pain he was obviously in. I knew Patrick did not understand why I was doing this to him. What could have been a quick diaper change was now a long, drawn out struggle between his strong will to satisfy his craving and my equally strong will to clean his bottom. I knew it hurt, but at the same time, I knew it would take away the cause of his pain. The diaper rash ointment I was trying to put on him would stop the pain and help prevent further pain. The crackers would do absolutely nothing for him except satisfy his immediate craving for food. "If only I could get this through to you," I thought, as I finally secured his new diaper in place with more electrical tape.

A short while later as I sat beside Patrick, with his pile of crackers stacked high on the table, I closed my eyes and began to pray. I was emotionally drained. During this little moment of silence, the Lord spoke to my heart about the troubles my strong will had caused me. I heard, "You are so much like Patrick, Beth. When I know something is hurting you—your bad habits, your sin—I want to wash it away, but you won't hold still. You kick and scream and say, 'If only it were the way I want, then the hurt would go away.' You won't let me take away the true cause of your pain. I want to wrap you in my grace to soothe the pain and prevent further damage, but all you can think of is feeding your hunger with things of this world. Then I want to wrap you in My Body to hold you together. If only you would stop complaining and kicking away all I send to you. Just rest in My divine will."

I opened my eyes and knew that the events that had just taken place with Patrick's diaper change were a gift from God. He had shown me exactly the way I act before Him. I continue to kick, pull away, and seek comfort in things of this world, but little by little I am learning to sit still.

I have changed many diapers since that day, and hope there will be more to come. Often, a little prayer comes to my heart now: "Lord, help me stop kicking and pulling away. Your will, not mine, be done today."

Do all things without grumbling or questioning, that you may be blameless and innocent, children of God without blemish in the midst of a crooked and perverse generation, among whom you shine as lights in the world.

—Philippians 2:14-15

Chapter Three

Innocent Suffering

December 15, 1999

My dear Patrick,

We are all so excited that you will be home soon for Christmas break. The kids are counting the days. I know, as always, the kids will gather around you, wanting to hug you and trying to get you to talk to them. They miss you so much. We will be putting our tree up soon, so it will be ready when you get here. I know how much you love to turn off all the lights in the house and sit by the fire looking at the Christmas tree all lit up with twinkling lights. Sometimes you get so excited that you jump up and dance around the room in delight. Over the past few years, you have even started to enjoy opening your Christmas presents. Your favorite gifts have always been figures from your favorite movies.

I pray this first trip home will not be too hard on you. I don't know how to help you understand that you are not coming home to stay. When we talk to you about things, you don't seem to understand a word we are saying. My heart is filled with joy that our home will once again know the happiness and laughter that only you can bring, and at the same time I feel pain when I think of the day when you will leave us and return to school. It is so hard to see you cry.

I can't think of anything harder for parents than to see their child suffer, and yet, God loved us so much that He gave us His only Son to suffer and die so that we could be His children. No matter what happens, Patrick, you will always be a child of God. No one can take that from you. It is your Christmas gift from God. God bless you, my little one.

I love you,
Mommy

[A]nd a sword will pierce through your own soul also,
that thoughts out of many hearts may be revealed.

—Luke 2:35

J have always found pain very hard to accept, especially when it is a child who suffers. I've wondered, "How can an all-loving God allow this? Why won't He take the pain away?" We have all seen the faces of weeping children clinging to their mothers in war-torn refugee camps and the dark, pain-stricken eyes of the Romanian orphans lying in their cribs. I used to question, "Why? How can this be?" God helped me to understand. He prepared me for all that I would go through with Patrick. He used my little, ten-month-old daughter Megan to teach me this lesson.

The drive to the emergency room seemed to go on forever, even though we lived only five minutes from Saint Vincent Carmel Hospital. I worked there as a nurse and had made the drive many times, but today I could not get there fast enough. As I looked toward the back seat, I could see my little baby Megan, so pale and motionless. I could not tell if she was breathing. I began to pray, "Please, Lord, don't take her now. Keep her alive. We're almost there." I rushed her into the emergency room and began to explain to the nurse what had happened, and then again to the doctor.

Megan had been fussy with a low-grade fever for the past few days. She awakened frequently during the night to nurse. I assumed she was teething and didn't think much of it. She was asleep when I left for Mass that Sunday morning. I knew I would be home later than usual because I was helping with the youth group's bake sale following Mass. When I returned home a few hours later, Mark was standing in the kitchen with Megan. She was not crying. She just lay there in his arms and moaned. He said that she had thrown up in her bed, and he could not get her to drink anything.

She had eaten about eight hours previously, and I decided she just needed to nurse. She refused, and as I held her, I could tell that her fever was up. I knew I had to get her to the hospital as quickly as possible. The nurses tried repeatedly to start an IV in her little arms. I watched painfully. She was so dehydrated that they could not find a vein. As I held my little baby, I could feel God holding me. She looked at me with eyes full of pain. The eyes spoke the question, "Why? Why are you letting them do this to me?"

Then I heard the Lord speak to me in my heart: "I have to, because I love you." I wanted to tell my daughter these words that the Lord was speaking to me. Just then I knew that through any pain He would hold me in the same way I was holding Megan. He would let me suffer only because He loves me even more than I love her. The doctors treated Megan for meningitis and sent her home a week later without a trace of the illness. All that is left is what I hold in my heart: "I have to, because I love you," the words my heavenly Father spoke to me that day as He held me.

Patrick has suffered much pain. At one point a doctor in Milwaukee told us that Patrick was in moderate to severe pain most of the time. Everything in his world irritated him. Every fabric, every sound, every touch, every taste. With the exception of dry carbohydrates, sugar, and water, everything irritated Patrick. He loves dry cereal and bread. He craves sugar. Patrick is happiest when he is under water. The water takes away all the things in his world that cause him pain.

I remember taking Patrick to the mall when he was about three years old. The minute we walked through the door, he began to giggle hysterically. While he was giggling and throwing himself on the floor, he would clench his fist very tightly. I could not get him to walk or to stop laughing. I had to carry him while I shopped. Once we left the mall, he was fine. Patrick frequently would have these laughing attacks and would throw himself on the floor, on a nearby couch, on Mark, or on me. Sometimes he would cry inconsolably for hours at a time. He would come to me with big crocodile tears flowing down his face, wanting to be held, only to pull away again. "Was I holding too tight, or not tightly enough? Was it my clothes, or the smell of my hair?" I never knew for sure.

I was comforted to think that even though he had his moments of crying, Patrick appeared to be a happy little guy for the most part. When I asked the autism specialist about his laughing fits, she told me something that God had prepared me to hear, but which was still very hard to hear. She said that Patrick is laughing because the situation is so stressful that he can't cry. Laughing and crying are so closely related that some people don't know which to do; often they laugh rather than cry. As her words came to my ears, the Father's words came to my heart: "I will only let you suffer because I love you." It broke my heart to think of all the times I had allowed lights, sounds, or some other stimuli to cause him so much pain, thinking he was enjoying them. I hoped that the specialist was wrong, but as I watched Patrick over time, I knew she was right. When I looked closely enough, I could see that sometimes when he laughed he was truly happy, but usually he was in pain. As a mother, I had to accept the fact that I would make mistakes in caring for this special little child.

I still questioned what good could possibly come from the suffering of an innocent child. One day God spoke to my heart again and let me know that He allows Patrick to suffer for reasons that we not only cannot see, but also cannot understand. I then recalled a story a friend once told me. Three poor travelers set off on a journey to another land. As they started on their way a voice spoke to them from the sky. They heard, "Pick up every rock you see along the way, and at the end of your journey, you will be both very happy and very sad." Eager to obey the voice, they quickly began to pick up every rock they saw and put it in their bags. Soon the bags became very heavy. They found themselves stepping over stones that they were too lazy or too tired to pick up. At other times they would complain about how heavy their bags were and would stop to take out the biggest rocks to lighten the load. Picking up the rocks became such a burden for them, that by the time they arrived at their destination, they could not wait to get rid of the bags that had caused them so much trouble. Their backs ached as they sat down on the bench to dump out the stones. As they opened their bags, they were filled with both great joy and great sadness, for the stones in their bags had turned to gold! They were filled with joy, for the stones that they carried the full length of the journey had turned to gold, but they were also very sad to think of the many rocks they had passed by or cast aside because they were just too difficult to carry a long way. Patrick is helping me to understand the value of picking up the rocks and carrying them on our journey, knowing there is an eternal promise with each one.

Will you question me about my children,
or command me concerning the work of my hands?

—Isaiah 45:11

CHAPTER FOUR

Into the Deep End

January 10, 2000

My dear Patrick,

I often see Daddy crying. He misses you so much. You are his little buddy. You have spent so much time with Daddy, just the two of you. It's usually in the car on an errand for Mommy. For so long, Daddy has been the only one strong enough to hold you when you are upset or hurting. He wants so much to hold you now.

I remember so well when you were little, about two, sitting on Daddy's lap. It was one of your favorite places to be, especially when he was reading the paper. He would start to read an article, then you would turn the page. I asked him how he could read the paper that way. With a smile, he said, "I just read whatever Patrick turns to, and when he turns the page I read something else."

Daddy is the one who always got to hold you at Mass and comfort you when the lights or noise bothered you. It was not unusual for the two of you to miss entire weddings, like your Aunt Patty and Uncle Jim's. During the wedding, you walked all through the beautiful Immaculata in San Diego. I'm sure you and Daddy saw parts of the church few people have seen.

Last summer, when Daddy took you to see the doctor in Los Angeles, it was just the two of you again. He knew the trip would be very hard on you with all the strange noises and people, so he took you somewhere he knew you would love. He took you to the Pacific Ocean. Do you remember that? There was water as far as you could see. I know Daddy treasures the memory of holding your hand and walking along the beach. He longs to hold your hand now, to hold his little buddy in his arms. We miss you so much. God bless you, my little one.

I love you,
Mommy

[I]t is the Spirit himself bearing witness with our spirit that we are children of God, and if children, then heirs, heirs of God and fellow heirs with Christ, provided we suffer with him in order that we may also be glorified with him.

—Romans 8:16-17

Little did I know that warm summer night when I went to bed that I would awaken to the sound of my husband drowning. In fact, only God knew—God and Patrick, that is. Patrick was five and full of surprises.

It had been a warm evening, and my husband, Mark, went to bed late. After checking on all the children and making sure they were all sound asleep, he lay down in bed with a book and a large glass of ice water. After a short period of reading, he turned off the light and fell soundly asleep. He was totally worn out from painting houses all day. A few hours later, I awoke to what sounded like a person drowning beside me. It was not a dream, and very quickly it became apparent to me what had happened. Patrick had awakened during the night and had gone in search of something to drink. He must have found his daddy asleep with his mouth open and decided to give him a drink. Patrick had tried to pour the entire glass of ice water down his daddy's throat. You can imagine what that would do to a person in the midst of a deep sleep, or anytime for that matter. As Mark tried to recover from the shock, and I reached for the light, there stood Patrick with a look of wonder on his face and his big, dark eyes questioning all the commotion. The glass still in his hand, he simply turned and walked out of the room.

Like me, Patrick has always loved water, or any liquid for that matter—the more, the better. When he was a small child, he would stand with a gallon of milk and just pour it out on the carpet. The entire time his eyes would never leave the flow of milk coming from the carton. Eventually, we had to put a lock on the refrigerator to keep him from pouring out every drink in the house. (You would think it would have been a great diet aid, but it only kept Patrick out, not my husband or me.)

One of Patrick's favorite activities is to fill one of our bathtubs to the brim and then swim around like a dolphin with big waves going over the top. He does not believe in turning the water off, so it has been common to find a flood of water flowing down the hall. We tried several times to give him swimming lessons, but he always preferred to sit at the bottom of the pool at the deepest end until he couldn't hold his breath anymore. Then he would come up for a breath and go right back to the bottom. This, as you can imagine, drove lifeguards and other parents crazy. We could not teach him to swim, but he taught himself to get around in the water fairly well. He is happiest when he is gliding through the water, swimming in his special way.

Patrick's love for water frequently reminds me of a story I once heard of a swimming instructor trying to teach a young child to swim. The child stood beside the pool as his teacher tried to convince him to come into the water. The child finally agreed to sit on the side of the pool, but he could not bring himself actually to get in. The teacher promised to hold him, and after awhile the child reluctantly agreed to get in, but only if he could hold on to the side of the pool.

All the while, the teacher continued to tell him that he would hold him and teach him to swim. He told the child how wonderful it would be to glide through the water with great speed. With fear in his eyes, the child let go of the side. He wanted so much to know the joy of racing through the water, but as he let go of the side of the pool, he could not let go of his fear of the water. So the little boy picked up a very small stone. To him it was just a little rock, something to remind him of the wall. It would be there for him if he needed it, if his teacher could not hold him.

At this point, the teacher held the child and said, "I cannot teach you to swim. That stone you have tightly in your hand can't hold you up, but it will make it impossible to swim. For you see, with a stone in your hand, you have paralyzed half of your body. You will never know the wonder of gliding through the water at great speed." Now, with his teacher's arms around him, he let go of the stone, and he watched as it fell to the bottom of the pool. He was ready to swim.

Because I was on a swimming team as a young girl, I knew the importance of using both hands to move through the water. How hard it would be with even a tiny stone in your hand! Many times in my life, I, like this child, have tried to cling to just one little stone, just one little area where I can still hold on. But God wants to teach me to swim. He is not asking me to swim the white-water rapids or dive into Niagara Falls. He is only asking me to get into the pool. As Patrick plays in the bath, the pool, or the creek, he reminds me that to experience the joy of life that God has in store for us, we must let go of the little rocks and let Him teach us to swim.

One of the little stones that I hold on to is my need for order and cleanliness. Little by little, God has used Patrick to pry open my fingers and drop the stone. My prayer has been, "Lord, your will be done, as long as things stay clean and orderly." I can remember studying child psychology in nursing school. There I sat at my desk just fascinated by how children can be taught how to act and by how they will respond. I would sit there daydreaming and plan exactly how my own future children would behave. I would have the perfect children. My home would be neat and orderly with everything in its proper place. And why not? It's just a matter of teaching the children the proper way to behave. To me this was the key, and I could not for the life of me figure out why no one else knew it.

God must have been smiling down on me with the gentle eyes of an all-knowing Father, for He knew that He would bless me with Patrick, a child who follows almost no directions or rules. Mother Teresa is quoted as saying, "If you want to make the heavenly Father laugh, tell Him your plans." I'm sure He has chuckled often.

For by grace you have been saved through faith; and this is not your own doing, it is the gift of God—not because of works, lest any man should boast. For we are his workmanship, created in Christ Jesus for good works, which God prepared beforehand, that we should walk in them.

—Ephesians 2:8-10

CHAPTER FIVE

Quick Compassion

February 18, 2000

My dear Patrick,

It was wonderful to come during the week to visit you. As always, it is saying good-bye to you that is so hard. I'm sure you were confused by the way we just showed up after class, took you out to dinner, and then left. You didn't seem to understand that we were only there for a conference with the school staff and could only stay for awhile.

The conference went well. They all really seem to care about you, and they are trying their best to help you in any way they can. God always seems to surround you with loving, kind people who see you as the precious gift that you are. Everyone commented about how affectionate you are and about your beautiful, dark eyes. I miss your eyes and your hugs. I miss everything about you, but most of all, I miss not being there to hold you when you cry.

You were so upset when we took you back to school. I was glad we took you out when we did. Do you remember the bad storm that hit while we were there? It made us feel as if we should leave early to get home, but we decided to stay. While we were at dinner with you, there was a fire at the school. Fortunately, the fire was under control very quickly, but I'm sure you would have been in a lot of pain from the alarms.

Once again the ride home was very hard on us. When we got home, the kids all wanted to know how you were. They love you so much, and it's very hard for them to understand why you had to leave. We pray for you every day, Patrick. God bless you, my little one.

I love you,
Mommy

Do not judge by appearances, but judge with right judgment.

—*John 7:24*

I was seated with my children in the back pew, and I could see that the church was full. It was an all-school Mass, with standing room only in the back. I was struggling to get Megan into her baby seat when my attention was drawn to the front of the church. There at the podium, a second or third grader was trying to finish the second reading, while many students in the pews giggled and pointed fingers at him. At that moment, the priest stood up and made his way toward the boy, but then he walked right past him. To my dismay, he then reached down and picked up my son Patrick, who was making his way toward the altar.

I was horrified. I could not imagine how he got away from me and all the way up to the front of the church. A moment before, I would have told you that my child would never do such a thing. Now, here was Father with Patrick in his arms. As someone walked Patrick back to me, Father mistakenly said, "I guess the little Martin boy wanted to concelebrate Mass with me." I was in the clear. "Now the entire congregation won't think it was a Matthews child who was not being properly cared for during Mass," I thought to myself, as the red slowly began to fade from my cheeks.

"If it truly had been another mother's child, would I have been quick to judge her parenting skills?" I wondered. Before Patrick, I would have answered yes. With many little tricks up his sleeve, Patrick has carried me a long way from where I was then. One of his favorite tricks has been showing up for Sunday Mass without any shoes on. He always has shoes on when we leave the house. Sometimes I wonder if our van eats shoes, because they are nowhere to be found when we get to church. Now, his lack of shoes doesn't bother me anymore; I just thank God if he doesn't chew open another ink pen on the way to Mass. (Ink from head to toe can really draw a lot of unwanted attention.)

Patrick thinks nothing of stealing someone's food or drink. When we go to a fast-food restaurant, we have to watch him closely, especially if anyone has chips or French fries, two of his favorites. He has gotten much better about this, but there was a time when he would not hesitate to swipe a doughnut as a stranger was putting it in his mouth. He didn't seem to care who the stranger was or what he was eating or drinking. If he wanted it, he took it. I have witnessed many stunned, hungry people standing with their mouths open, wondering what just happened to them. Usually a quick apology and explanation were enough to make things right again, but not always.

When Patrick was about seven, he took a bag of chips from a little boy at our local pool. The boy, who was sitting with his mother, began to cry. I quickly ran to grab Patrick and return the chips, but the mother appeared to be angry at me and did not seem the least bit interested in hearing my apology or an explanation. I said what I had to say, and then I took Patrick's hand and walked away somewhat irritated at this woman's lack of understanding. I judged her harshly for obviously not being able to see that I was trying and that Patrick didn't know any better. As the irritation was growing inside me, the woman approached me, and now it was my turn to listen. She said, "I'm so sorry. I know I was short with you, but I was in shock. Someone threw a lawn chair through the window of my car, and I had just bought my son the chips to calm him down while I tried to figure out what to do next. Please don't worry about the chips. It's really no trouble at all." I smiled and thanked her, wishing I could take back all the unkind thoughts that had passed through my mind in those few minutes.

"Why am I so quick to judge and think others just don't understand?" I asked myself. Over the years, I have found the answer: It's because we don't walk in one another's shoes. I don't understand because I *can't* fully understand. I can never know what it's like to live the life of another or have to make the decisions another has had to make. I have never had to be a mother to their children. I can understand some of the struggles of a mother with an autistic child, but two autistic children can be as different as night and day. I have nine fairly well-behaved children, and I have one child who is very difficult. He follows very few rules of society, often screams to get what he wants, throws himself on the ground, and sometimes kicks and hits. Some of my friends have many children who are very difficult to handle. At this point, I have only one such child, and he happens to be autistic. He does not wear a sign that says "I'm autistic." I don't even think a sign would help stop the stares.

One thing is certain. A child's inappropriate behavior does not always mean a lack of good parenting skills. I don't know how many times I've heard, "What that child needs is a good spanking," and many similar words of advice.

Once, when Patrick was about three, I was trying to lead a mothers' group at Our Lady of Mount Carmel Church. Patrick was very upset in the baby-sitting room, and I could hear him crying. I decided to leave the meeting and see what I could do to help calm Patrick. As I closed the door and turned around, there was Patrick, happy and giggling in the arms of one of his favorite priests, Father Dan Gartland. Patrick has always loved men in black, especially with a Roman collar. Father told me to go back to my meeting. He would take care of Patrick. When I inquired about his appointments that morning, he said that he'd be fine. He was right. When I entered his office awhile later to pick up Patrick, there was Father Dan with Patrick sound asleep in his arms.

Another priest, Father Richard Doerr, once went to great lengths to help when Patrick's world seemed to have turned upside down. To most, it may not have seemed like such a big deal; but to Patrick, Mark, and me, it was a nightmare. Sharp Tooth, Patrick's beloved dinosaur, which he carried everywhere with him, was missing. We searched the yard with a flashlight on many nights to find the toy, because Patrick wouldn't go to bed without it. It was part of a limited collection of *The Land before Time* characters. We had searched the house and then the neighborhood, but still we couldn't find it anywhere. Sean and Laura drew pictures of Sharp Tooth and made signs to pass out. As you can imagine, Patrick was not happy. He walked around the house crying, and we could only guess that he was looking for his favorite tyrannosaurus, Sharp Tooth.

When Father Richard heard about the missing dinosaur, knowing that Patrick was rarely seen without it, he and his younger brother went on a mission to find another one. Soon Father Richard was at our door with a new dinosaur just like the other one. He explained that a relative had the entire collection and yet was willing to give up her Sharp Tooth if it would help. Once again, Patrick and his tyrannosaurus ruled the house.

God has used Patrick to help me see that when another parent or friend is struggling, I need to hold my tongue and offer my hand and my heart. A prayer is the greatest gift I can give a parent, followed by an encouraging smile and an offer to help.

Behold, I have graven you on the palms of my hands.

—*Isaiah 49:16*

CHAPTER SIX

Count It All Joy

March 2, 2000

My dear Patrick,

We all miss you so much. The weather has started to warm up a bit, and it seems the kids cannot decide if they want to be in or out. You are not the only one who challenges my efforts to keep the house clean. The flow of muddy shoes is endless as your brothers and sisters spend countless hours running in the field, climbing trees, or playing on the swings.

I miss not seeing you out there with them. I love sitting in my rocking chair on the porch watching you try to play with the kids. I can remember last summer when Sean was trying to teach you to play basketball. You tried to shoot a few times, but then it was off to the swings. You always seem so happy on the swings. I think that is why your brothers and sisters like to be on the swings with you so much. Your happiness makes them happy. Every day, at least one of them asks me when you will be home.

I hope you are able to spend time playing outside when it's warm enough. The playground there is so nice. Maybe we can play outside this weekend when we come for a visit, and Daddy will push you on the swing. Do you remember the swing that Daddy and our friend Caesar put up in the garage at our house in Carmel? Caesar had someone weld a special piece of steel so that your swing would work just right. We would always listen for the sound of the swing in the garage and know that rain or shine, you were happy on the swing. I fight back the tears as my arms ache to hold you. We miss you. God bless you, my little one.

I love you,
Mommy

*Blessed is the man who endures trial, for when he has
stood the test he will receive the crown of life
which God has promised to those who love him.*

—James 1:12

I derive a great deal of satisfaction from making out a list, setting up a plan of action, following through, and then seeing the results. My problem is the pride that comes along with accomplishing the task. Time and again, God has used Patrick to humble me and help me to realize that without His grace, I could not have even put together the list in the first place. Those who are closest to me have seen how I can turn my plan of action into my own personal, little god—and beware to anyone who gets in the way of what I intend to accomplish!

This is most evident to me in my cleaning projects. We start with scrubbing the corners of the closets and then move toward the center. Spring cleaning is a big project, but for me it is not enough. I have yet to come up with the perfect plan, so I just continue with one major cleaning flowing into another. We have "get ready for school" cleaning in the fall, "pre- and post-Thanksgiving and Christmas" cleanings, "a warm day, so let's clean the garage" cleaning, and "I can't go to sleep until the bathrooms are clean" cleaning. Then there is always the "before the baby comes" cleaning, and the greatest of them all, the postpartum cleaning.

Each time I am blessed with new life, I have had my activity restricted, to say the least. For the last six pregnancies, I have been told to stay off my feet during the last trimester; sometimes, I have even been on complete bed rest. I go through a three-to-four-month period of hearing "Oh, just let it go. It's only a house" and "Let someone else take care of that. You need to rest." I have had to lie on the couch and look at a large glob of grape jelly on the floor. "Doesn't anyone else see it?" I wonder. "Don't they know that once that jelly is on the bottom of a shoe, it is very hard to get off, and then it will spread through the house attached to a very active toddler who will leave a trail of sticky mess in each room?" That's not so bad until you think of the amount of dirt that will be attracted from miles away to come and stick to that glob of jelly that has moved through my house. Now, instead of one quick swipe with the washcloth, we are in need of a carpet cleaner. This can all race through my head in a split second, and people wonder why I can't just let it go. They don't live with Patrick.

All I can think of is "Someone wipe up the jelly, and while you're at it, I can think of a hundred other things that need to be done." Prevention may be important, but I truly believe that humility is the key. When I see myself as only an instrument and recognize that it is only by His grace that I can do anything, I find maintaining a household with ten children far less challenging. With Patrick's help, there came a time when God showed me that my true enemy was not the mess or the bed rest, but pride, pride in my own ability.

It was spring-cleaning time, and what a sense of accomplishment I had! I marveled that I had been able to get every kitchen cabinet cleaned. I cleaned out each crack and cranny. That evening, God gave me the opportunity to practice two very important virtues: humility and joy. This opportunity required what Mark and I call "giving it the old one-two," in other words, James 1:2, which reads, "Count it all joy, my brethren, when you meet various trials." I had gone to the store and returned with some two-liter pop bottles for the retreat meeting we were having that night. I had left the bottles on the counter and gone into the living room for just a brief moment, when I heard an explosive sound followed by fizzing. As I entered the kitchen, I could see Patrick, happy as he could be, with a Coke bottle in his hand and fizz spraying all over the kitchen. Sticky Coke was everywhere, in every crack and crevice. He must have shaken it well because there was almost nothing left in the bottle. Mark and I smiled at each other, and then, as usual, one of us took Patrick, and the other began to clean. I was beginning to learn that what we have done for God cannot be undone, even by a little child with an explosive pop bottle, but obviously I needed more practice.

Early one morning, I was awakened by the sound of Patrick downstairs in the kitchen. This was not unusual. He would awaken at the crack of dawn many mornings. My main concern was that he would not go back to sleep and that I would be subjected to sitting through another viewing of Patrick's all-time favorite movie, *Chitty Chitty Bang Bang*. Once Patrick is awake, someone has to be up with him, or there is no telling what he will do. Mark and I had memorized all two and a half hours of the movie, and as much as I like Dick Van Dyke, I was not looking forward to the one hundredth rendition of "Me Old Bamboo."

My dread of the movie turned into shock when I saw what was in front of me. After I picked up my jaw from the floor, I asked myself, "Just how much is in one of those cake mix boxes?" My dining room looked as if it had been hit by a snowstorm. Old oak furniture and cake mix do not go well together. Each crack and groove was now white, and the more I cleaned, the worse it seemed to get. (If you think cake mix is bad, you can only imagine what he did with a two-pound bag of powdered sugar one Christmas. Let's just say there wasn't much left for baking cookies.) Even with locks on the cabinets, Patrick never runs out of ideas for ways to help me grow in virtue.

> *Because you are precious in my eyes, and honored,*
> *and I love you, I give men in return for you,*
> *peoples in exchange for your life.*

> —*Isaiah 43:4*

CHAPTER SEVEN

A Clean Soul

March 14, 2000

My dear Patrick,

The months go by, and it hasn't gotten any easier. It does not take much to start tears flowing from the eyes of your daddy or me. It seems so wrong to have you so far away from home, and yet we trust that God will use all this suffering for His honor and glory.

During this season of Lent, I have looked to our Mother Mary as never before. She endured such great pain at seeing her beautiful, innocent Son suffer and die on the Cross, and yet she trusted in the will of God. Patrick, all the pain you are enduring is not wasted. It is united with the suffering of Christ on the Cross for the salvation of the world. Like Mary, I must give you to God and believe that your life is not just a blessing for our family, but a special blessing for the entire world. Yes, Patrick, in some small way I can feel a portion of the pain Mary suffered. How her arms must have ached to hold her Son! How her heart must have ached to see Him in such pain! It's pain He endured for my sin.

With Mary's pain, there also had to be a joy in knowing that on the Cross, Christ honored and glorified the Father. He gave Himself completely. Daddy and I gave you back to God the day your life was revealed to us. We continue to place your life in God's hands each day in our constant prayer for you and each night in our family Rosary. Patrick, Daddy and I believe that in your life you have not been capable of committing a sin deliberately and with understanding. This is a beautiful thing, and it gives us great comfort to sustain us in these times of so much pain. We miss you so much. God bless you, my little one.

I love you,
Mommy

I can do all things in him who strengthens me.

—*Philippians 4:13*

God knew better than to place me in an immaculately clean home, the kind I had always dreamed of. In His infinite wisdom, He knew that the best way to draw me to Himself was to bring me to my knees, in prayer, several times a day. Patrick has always been more than happy to be God's little helper, always finding new and exciting ways to bring me to my knees. At a very young age, Patrick not only poured liquids on the carpet, but he also discovered that eggs will crack on carpet if you drop them hard enough and that eggs will crack under the cushions of chairs when you sit on them.

Eggs are only one item in a long list of substances I have cleaned off floors. Others include orange juice, paint, glue, ink, pizza sauce, and liquid soap, to mention a few. I know many parents have to deal with youngsters who don't share their desires for clean carpets and counters, but Patrick took this challenge of messing things up to a higher level. Mother Teresa said once, "Every day at Communion time, I communicate two of my feelings to Jesus. One is gratefulness because He has helped me to persevere until today. The other is a request. Teach me to pray."[1] I have Patrick to thank for the many hours I've spent on my knees cleaning floors, but God used Patrick not only to teach me to pray, but also to give me many opportunities to do my cleaning cheerfully and offer it to Him.

Take, for instance, a beautiful fall morning several years ago. It was one of those mornings when—I have to admit—I was feeling as if I had everything under control. I had a load of laundry in the washer and decided to prepare dinner to go

---

[1] *Mother Teresa: In My Own Words* (New York: Gramercy Books, 1997), 11.

into the Crock Pot before cleaning the kitchen from breakfast. There was very little to do in the kitchen—just loading a few dishes in the dishwasher and putting the cereal away. The night before, I had scrubbed the white tile kitchen floor. I had Mark install a white floor so I could always see when it was dirty. (I know better now.) Things were looking pretty good that morning. Suddenly, Patrick came prancing into the kitchen, grabbed the extra-large box of Cheerios from the counter and took one handful. He then dropped the box on the floor before running from the kitchen.

The entire contents of the box spilled onto the floor in every direction. It looked like a carpet of Cheerios. At this time, I had seven young children moving about the house, but I kept calm and thought to myself, "No big deal. Cheerios are easy to sweep up. I'll finish getting dinner into the Crock Pot and then move on to the Cheerios." I delayed my actions. As I turned to continue preparing dinner, Patrick came in to remind me, I think, of the importance of not putting off until later what needs to be done now. Patrick reached for a large glass of orange juice, took a very quick drink, and went to set it on the table. Yet somehow he missed the table by an inch and the entire glass of orange juice tumbled to the floor. As I watched it fall, it seemed to be floating in midair, almost teasing me. It was as if the orange juice were saying, "I'm going to land on the floor. There is nothing you can do to stop me. Now what are you going to do?" It was like one of those scenes from a movie when the camera slows down to show everything in minute detail. Cheerios are easy to clean, but Cheerios in a large puddle of orange juice splattered across the floor—that's another story.

At this point, as six kids came into the kitchen to see what the noise was, I thanked God for all my experience as a cardiac nurse. With the grace of God, I was able to move into what I call triage mothering. I was able to get all six children, except

Patrick, to remove their juice-covered shoes and sit on the sofa to read. On my knees, I then slowly began to clean the juice-soaked Cheerios from the floor and carpet. While cleaning the floor, I asked the Lord the question that I ask in this sort of situation. I asked Him, "Lord, what am I learning?"

Suddenly, my mind was filled with thoughts of cleaning our souls. I thought of how one small sin doesn't seem like much, and we can so easily convince ourselves that it won't hurt to take care of it later. But oh, the trouble it can cause! And how it can lead to even greater sin! Then what a mess we may have to face.

I smiled as I cleaned the floor. The Lord used my little Patrick to show me the importance of Confession. He was telling me to strive for immaculate cleanliness in His home, my soul. He was also telling me that He would provide, as always, the grace I would need.

For everything created by God is good, and
nothing is to be rejected if it is received with thanksgiving;
for then it is consecrated by the word of God and prayer.

—*1 Timothy 4:4-5*

CHAPTER EIGHT

The Carnival Mirror

April 22, 2000

My dear Patrick,
  Happy birthday! Today was filled with so much joy and yet so much pain. It's hard to believe it's been eleven years since you were born. Today we celebrated your birthday with you. The joy in spending the day with you and the pain when it came time to leave you were so great that I wonder if I will ever stop crying.
  You loved your birthday cake, with Winnie the Pooh dressed as the Easter Bunny. You knew the minute we began to sing "Happy Birthday," and your smile lit up the room. You were even able to blow out all eleven candles. That in itself is such a struggle for you. Your favorite gift was the movie Charlotte's Web. *The other children began to watch it, but I promised you could watch it later because we wanted to take you to the zoo.*
  It was a beautiful day to walk through the zoo with our whole family together again. You loved watching the sea lions swimming back and forth in their pool. I'm sure you wanted to join them, and that's why Daddy and Sean kept a tight hold on your hand at all times.
  Little did we know when we took you back to school today that we would experience so much pain. We knew the pain of having you pull on our hands, since you wanted to stay with us. We knew the pain of seeing your tears and hearing you cry, but today we felt a new pain. When we returned to the school, I stopped your crying by reminding you that you had Charlotte's Web *and could watch it when we returned.*

Immediately, you stopped crying and ran down the hall toward the recreation room. The staff changed while we were at the zoo, and the new staff refused to let you watch your movie. One staff member would not even look at me when I tried to explain that you had been told you could watch your birthday movie when we returned. How could I stand there and let someone hurt you like that? I began to regret that I even gave you the movie. The longer we stayed, the more you cried. Finally, we realized that it would be best for us to go. For so many years, I have eased your pain by letting you watch your favorite movies. Today, my hands were tied.

When we got home, I called the school. They told me you were very happy watching Charlotte's Web. *You were happy, but my eyes are filled with tears. For the first time in eleven years, I cannot give you a birthday kiss good night. Even though I cannot hold you in my arms, Patrick, I hold you in my heart and, with Daddy, I thank God for the precious gift of your life. God bless you, my little one.*

I love you,
Mommy

I appeal to you therefore, brethren, by the mercies of God, to present your bodies as a living sacrifice, holy and acceptable to God, which is your spiritual worship.

—*Romans 12:1*

Have you ever looked at yourself in a carnival mirror, the kind that makes you look short and fat or very tall and thin, and then decided to go on a diet because of what you saw? I hope not. We all know that what we see is a distortion of what is really there. I don't know of anyone who has been upset by what he saw in a carnival mirror. It is usually an occasion for a good laugh and nothing more.

Unfortunately, it took me years to realize that the image I saw of myself was distorted just as badly. Many things distorted the image before my eyes when I looked in a mirror. The distortion started with the dolls I played with as a child (they had "perfect" bodies) and continued with my fellow cheerleaders in high school, who were always thinner than I was, and the beautiful airbrushed images of the women on the covers of magazines. At five feet eight inches and 130 pounds, I dreamed of being thinner. No matter how thin I was, my legs were never thin enough.

After I delivered my first child, Sean, I came home from the hospital in my jeans. This was something I was very proud of, and I tucked away for safekeeping all the comments about how good I looked after just having a baby. With my second child, Laura, I was back to 130 pounds at my six-week, postpartum checkup. Once again, I loved all the comments about how good I looked. It was easy to equate "thin" with "good." After the checkup, my weight loss did not end at 130 pounds. By the time Laura was nine months old, my weight had dropped to 118 pounds. It was great. I could wear anything I wanted without being afraid of how I looked. My brother's wedding was that summer, and we had ordered a size-fourteen dress for fear that I wouldn't lose the baby weight in time. It had to be altered to a size eight. I was finally as thin as I had ever wanted to be.

Then Patrick took it all away from me. From the day I brought Laura home from the hospital, I began to pray for and long for another baby. In my heart, I knew I would have another child, and we would name him Patrick. I longed for Patrick more than Sean and Laura. This was not because I did not love them—on the contrary, it was because I loved them so much. Before Sean was born, I had not yet tasted such joy, and he was eight weeks old when God blessed us with Laura's life inside of me. The beautiful gift of their lives

was something I treasured so dearly, and I could not wait to share the precious gift of life with another child. After months of waiting, a baby was once again growing inside me.

I knew what pregnancy does to my hips. They triple in size. But I told myself that this time would be different. I was right. It was very different. Patrick smashed through my carnival image of myself. I gained sixty pounds in nine months. I felt like a large, beached whale. I still had all the comments about how I looked so good tucked away in my mind. I knew they would not apply this time. He was born in the spring, and none of my summer clothes fit. Even my maternity clothes were too tight. I had just come from the hospital, and nothing I owned seemed to fit. Finally, I settled on a large pair of maternity shorts and an extra-large T-shirt of Mark's. Just as I finished dressing, Mark entered the room. Standing there in shorts made me so self conscious of how I looked, but before I could say anything, he looked at me and said, "Beth, you look so much better than you did last summer before you had Patrick, when you were all skin and bones." At that, he walked back out of the room. He left me standing there in shock. All my bony limbs were covered in the soft, round curves of motherhood, and he loved the way I looked. In that one comment, he opened my eyes to all the lies I had been fed by society. The distorted image vanished, and when I turned and looked in the mirror, I saw for the first time what God wanted me to see—the soft, round, mommy figure that had come with months of carrying Patrick.

The nausea, the pain from constant contractions throughout the pregnancy, the headaches, the fatigue—I had offered it all to God. The one thing I held back was my weight. I could not stand the thought of being overweight, but He said, "No." He wanted all of me, even my weight. In giving my body for the life of Patrick, God blessed me with the body I so dearly wanted: the body of a mother.

*[M]y frame was not hidden from thee, when I was being made
in secret, intricately wrought in the depths of the earth.
Thy eyes beheld my unformed substance; in thy book
were written every one of them, the days that were formed
for me, when as yet there was none of them.*

—*Psalm 139:15-16*

CHAPTER NINE

Not by Bread Alone

April 23, 2000

My dear Patrick,

Today is Easter, and how I wish you could have been here to share it with us! I know how much you have always loved watching the children hunt for candy and eggs. I can remember many times watching your brothers and sisters lead you around by the hand trying to help you find candy. You never have quite figured out that you eat what you find, so they have always been more than happy to share their candy with you. You have taught them so much about the true joy of giving.

Surrounded by the beauty of spring, we drove to Mass. There, in the presence of Christ in the Eucharist, I felt the joy and hope of the Resurrection. Patrick, Christ has shown us that it is in giving of ourselves that we receive, and in dying that we are born to eternal life. You have helped me to give and give and give, and with what great joy! Because of you, Patrick, my soul longs to receive the Eucharist, the Bread of Life that you may never be able to receive.

When our friends' children who are your age made their First Holy Communion, Daddy and I were very sad. We wanted so much for you to be with them. I was at a mothers' lunch, and the children who were preparing for First Communion came out to sing to the mothers. I couldn't hold back the tears, so I had to leave.

You have had to miss out on so many special occasions in your life. You've never played Little League or sung in a school play. You've never been invited to a birthday party or had a friend over to play. We take so many things like that for granted, but as usual, you have taught us that those kinds of things don't matter so much. Your daddy and I never had those kinds of plans for you when you were born. Sure, it would be nice if you could play with friends or be on a baseball team, but what is more important is that you are with Christ. Even though you can't receive the Eucharist, you will be perfected in heaven. You are our special saint here on earth. Maybe the world doesn't recognize the beauty and holiness that you possess, but Daddy and I do. Thank you for being our beautiful son. God bless you, my little one.

I love you,
Mommy

———◆◇◆———

The Lord Jesus on the night when he was betrayed took bread, and when he had given thanks, he broke it, and said, "This is my body which is for you. Do this in remembrance of me."

—*1 Corinthians 11:23-24*

She stumbled through the kitchen in a manner reminiscent of someone in a state of dire deprivation. Gasping for a breath, she moaned in a slow, sad voice, "There's nothing to eat for breakfast." This was not a poor child in a shack with bare cupboards. Neither was she someone living in a Third World nation. No, this was someone in a modern kitchen stocked to the brim with food. When I dare to point out to my thirteen-year-old daughter, Laura, that there are ten boxes of cereal on the counter to choose from, she gives me a startled, deer-in-the-headlights look as if I had just told her to eat mud. (I choose not to mention to her the bread, butter, and homemade strawberry jam next to the toaster.) I can understand her point.

How many times in my life had I decided to go hungry rather than to eat something that my pallet did not prefer?

We were out of eggs and the kind of cereal Laura likes. In her mind, there was nothing to eat for breakfast. I left the kitchen with my cup of coffee and sat down in the living room for a moment of prayer.

Laura tries so hard to live her life for Christ; she tries to imitate every saint she reads about, but like her mother, this imitation usually does not extend to the area of food. I had to ask myself why. Why can't I use food as a gift from God for the nourishment of my body and not only for the sheer joy of eating? If I truly believed what I prayed before each meal with Mark and the children—"Bless us, O Lord, and these thy gifts," and the second prayer, "whether we eat or drink, do all for the honor and glory of God" (cf. 1 Corinthians 10:13)—then I needed to live it. I asked myself, "Does the way I eat give honor and glory to God, not just some of the time, but with each bite?" The answer was "No!" I began to pray, "Lord, help me to appreciate the food with which you bless me. With each meal, show me how to eat less of what I like, more of what I don't, and never more than what I need."

Just then, a noise came from the kitchen. My motherly ears knew it as the distinct sound of a utensil—probably a butter knife—falling to the floor. No more time to pray. Patrick was awake and in the kitchen trying to make toast. For Patrick, eating is definitely pleasurable at times, but it is also very difficult. As I watched him butter his toast carefully, something he had recently learned to do, my mind was filled with memories of the struggle Patrick has had with food. It took many years of trying before he was able to take his first bite of some of his favorite fare.

During Patrick's first year and a half of life, he ate anything that was served to him. He not only ate it, but ate it very quickly. I could not feed him fast enough. I remember once feeding mashed potatoes to one of my stroke patients, a tiny, fragile, elderly lady. Somehow between bites, she managed to gasp, "Please, please, could you slow down?" I was so used to feeding Patrick that I had forgotten that the rest of the world doesn't eat as fast.

Sometime during Patrick's second year of life, he stopped eating almost everything that was not dry carbohydrates. One of his favorite foods was Cheerios, and he would get very upset with me in the morning when I swept the kitchen floor. He would look at me as if I were crazy. It made no sense to him. Why would I take the time to sweep all these wonderful things, including the stash of Cheerios he had saved for later, into a big pile, only to put them in the trash? Along with Cheerios, crackers (especially whole wheat crackers), cookies, and bread made up his entire diet. Day after day we tried to introduce new foods, especially pizza, a family favorite, but he would only cringe and pull back in his chair when we put it near his mouth.

I was determined to make the foods he would eat as nutritious as possible. His cookies were usually oatmeal, made with honey and whole wheat flour, and I began to make only whole wheat bread. He loved the whole wheat bread, and I loved that he was eating at least something nutritious. He enjoyed the bread so much that he would not even wait for it to cool after I took it from the oven. The center of each loaf was usually gone before I had time to cut it. The other children became accustomed to rather strangely shaped sandwiches.

After years of failed attempts, Patrick finally decided that he would try the crust of a slice of pizza. He looked at it for what seemed like hours, brought it close to his mouth, and then cringed and turned his head away. He acted like a child who had been asked to eat a live cricket. Since that time, we have learned that many autistic children's senses are so acutely sensitive that they can see and taste things that we can't. "What is he seeing on that little crust of pizza that he just couldn't bring himself to put in his mouth?" I wondered. Then he began to pick at it. Little pieces of the crust had to be removed. Some had specks of sauce on them, but others looked no different to me from the rest of the crust. No matter, Patrick saw something he didn't like and had to eradicate it.

Then it happened. He took a small bite. As he chewed, his body cringed, and with the next small bite, his face was filled with a look of disgust. More little bits of crust had to be removed, and eventually he finished the entire piece. Over time, Patrick taught himself to tolerate the sauce, and then the cheese, and now pizza is one of his favorite foods. One of the greatest things about visiting Patrick at school is the opportunity to take him to his favorite pizza place. The pizza doesn't taste any better to us, but it is so much more enjoyable to go with Patrick, since we know that he enjoys it so much. He still looks at it from every angle and removes little bits of it before his first bite, but now it's nothing for him to eat six slices at one meal.

It was about the time that Patrick learned to eat pizza and apples—which I was elated about—that we were told by a specialist that his autistic behavior was caused by a candida yeast infection. After seeing Patrick, he told us that the yeast was feeding off the sugar in his diet, and he would need to go on a low carbohydrate, high protein diet, and a medication called nystatin. He told us that Patrick eventually would eat the protein. The doctor said that it was up to me to provide him with the correct foods, and when he was hungry enough, he would eat it.

My heart grew heavy as I watched Patrick trying every way he knew how to get to the foods we had always let him have so freely. He began climbing out windows. He even went out an upstairs window, across the gutter, over the garage roof, and from there dropped to the ground to get to food. He did not plan on our neighbor catching him and bringing him home. Patrick knew no fear when it came to getting to what his body most desired. With a year of no improvement in his behavior, and with our home turned upside down, we took him off the diet and medication, and let him once again eat the homemade bread and cookies that he loved.

Patrick sat at the table frantically eating his toast for fear I might take it away, and I realized that it had been over six years since we tried that first diet. Now we were at it again. Another doctor told us that if Patrick would stop eating the food he loved, his autistic behavior would improve. He also said that with a special diet, in combination with certain medications, he might even be healed. This was enough to get us to try it again, but at what cost to Patrick? We were told either to eliminate or to give only small portions of everything he liked. The exception was boneless, skinless chicken breast marinated in Italian dressing and cooked on an outside grill. The chicken had become one of his favorites, but it could not replace the bread.

I cannot imagine eating one meal with food I did not prefer, much less living on a diet with food that repulsed me, as the food Patrick was offered repulsed him. We replaced the home-made whole wheat bread that he loved with store-bought white bread, but that was only a few slices a day. A few slices were not enough to satisfy that craving for bread. I knew in a moment he would be back in the kitchen trying to make more toast. He would be trying to figure out why his mommy could no longer let him have the bread he loved so much.

I held my coffee cup and began to cry, but I also began to pray. At that moment, I saw how many times I have tried to make things right with tasty food and have told myself that I will feel better once I've eaten. Through my tears for Patrick, God spoke to my heart and reminded me that He is the bread I need. I saw that the only way I could honor and glorify God with food was to use it as the gift it was meant to be, to sustain my body. No matter what I ate or how much I ate, I knew it could not fill my soul. Only His Body can do that. I need to fill up on the Bread of Life, Christ, and not on homemade bread. Mark and I have always believed very strongly that Christ, especially in the Eucharist, strengthens and sustains our marriage. As I look back over the years, I can see that He was there, especially in the difficult times. He was there in the Eucharist, giving me the food I so dearly loved and needed most of all.

And she gave birth to her first-born son and
wrapped him in swaddling cloths, and laid him in a manger,
because there was no place for them in the inn.

—Luke 2:7

CHAPTER TEN

The Walls of Freedom

May 25, 2000

My dear Patrick,

We all miss you so very much. Summer is in the air, and everyone is glad to be done with school and outside playing. I'm sure you are spending more and more time outside after school, climbing on the jungle gym and swinging on the swings. I know how much you love to climb as high as you can get. Maybe someday Daddy can build you a tree house so you can climb up high and look out over the fields and woods.

Today our homeschooling group, Saint Monica's, went on a field trip at the end of the school year to Holiday World. I carried you in my heart the entire day. Everything we did reminded me of how much you would have loved it. So many of the rides go around and swing back and forth, but the place you would have loved the most is the waterpark. They have a wave pool that feels like the waves in the ocean, and giant slides that shoot water as you slide down into the pool. Every direction you look, there is another pool. I pray that someday soon we will be able to take you there for an entire day and let you swim in any pool you want.

I know what a struggle it has been for you to stay out of the pools in our neighborhood. I think your little body craves being in water the way a thirsty person desires to drink water—if only you could understand the danger, especially when you get in under the winter tarps. Because the pain of separation has been so great, I cannot imagine the pain of losing you. I cannot imagine never holding you in my arms again and looking into your beautiful, dark eyes. I know you are surrounded by many angels, and that gives me great comfort. God bless you, my little one.

I love you,
Mommy

*For the time is coming when people will not
endure sound teaching, but having itching ears
they will accumulate for themselves teachers to
suit their own likings, and will turn away from
listening to the truth and wander into myths.*

—*2 Timothy 4:3-4*

I stood there at the kitchen window and watched as
Patrick swung back and forth on his swing in the backyard. He looked so happy as he kicked his feet high into
the air. I could see the smile on his face, and, through the open
window, I could even hear him laugh. As I washed dishes, I
thought of the beauty of the fence that surrounded my little
Patrick and gave him the freedom to spend hours on the swing
in the backyard. Before the fence was built, he was a slave, a
slave to his desire to wander into danger. Before the fence was
built, Patrick would constantly stand at the door crying to go
outside, only to be told no because I knew that there was no
way I could keep up with him. If he slipped away, the dangers
that awaited him were great.

God gave us the fence. He provided the money and then
built it with the hands of His Mystical Body, the Church. It
was a beautiful sight to see all the men working side by side
building the fence. It was a Saturday morning, when each of
them could have been catching up on his own chores at home
or simply enjoying the pleasures of a crisp, clear autumn day.
None of them complained. They even seemed to enjoy it as
they compared various methods of leveling out sections of
fence post. Our friend, Caesar, created a leveling device with
plastic tubing and colored water. It was the envy of all the men
there. When the last board was nailed, Patrick raced for the
swing, and his freedom began.

For a few years, Patrick was able to run and play in the
backyard most of the time, but as he grew older and

stronger, he could climb to the top of his playhouse and see the world beyond the fence. The fence that had given him his freedom became an obstacle in his way, keeping him from what he wanted.

It all happened so suddenly, but then with Patrick things frequently happen suddenly. I left the kitchen for just a minute to check on the little ones, and when I went to the window again, Patrick was gone. "I didn't hear the door open," I thought to myself. I figured he had to be in the backyard somewhere. There was no way he could get over the fence. I could not see the gate from the window so I ran out the back door to the gate, and it was closed with the lock secure. At this point I figured he must have slipped past me into the house, so I frantically ran back into the house to continue my search. As I expected, the front door was locked securely, as were all the windows.

As I searched through the house, I tried to remain calm, but at the same time I was frightened. "Lord, please help me find Patrick," I prayed. It would be scary enough to have a five-year-old child missing, but the world held great dangers for a child like Patrick. There were many ponds and pools in the area, each of which Patrick would jump into without a second's thought. If he didn't go into the pools or ponds, there were busy roads nearby. He was very attracted to roads because he liked to lie on the road and look at how the line runs down the middle. While Mark played basketball in the driveway with the kids, Patrick would often run off to lie in the center of the street. Patrick had even tried to run in front of an oncoming car so that he could touch the shiny bumper. "What if he gets to the highway? It's only a few blocks away," I thought as I finished my second search of the house. I could not imagine how he got out, but I knew he was out there somewhere. After scanning the neighborhood from the upstairs windows, I notified several neighbors and called the police.

The response from everyone was wonderful. No one hesitated to search. They acted as if their own son were missing. After searching the house again and going over my story, the police took a few pictures of Patrick and began to canvass the area. I had hoped to be able to find Patrick without calling Mark out of class at school, but now I knew he had to come home to help.

In the meantime, nearly two miles away, Patrick had found an open house and decided to go in to find something to eat. The family who lived there was on vacation, and a relative who was staying at the house was out working in the yard. He came inside to find a strange boy drinking a Coke, eating an apple, and watching television. It became apparent to him very quickly that he was not going to get any information out of this little boy, so he took him outside where he hoped someone might recognize him.

A newspaper reporter heard the call over the police radio and decided to go after the story. The number of our address was 1115. We lived in a subdivision off 146th Street. Somehow, the reporter got the information wrong, thought he had heard "151" and not "1115," and was driving along 151st Street looking for our house. As he drove along, he saw a man standing by the road with a young boy and decided to stop to ask directions. The man told the reporter that he did not know the area, that he was from out of town. Then he went on to mention that he was looking for someone who might recognize the little boy with him because he wouldn't talk and seemed to be lost. The reporter told the man that he was looking for our house to do a story on a little boy who was missing. They quickly realized that this was the same boy. The reporter then phoned the police, and in no time, Patrick was returned safely home in a sheriff's car. Patrick was oblivious to all the fuss. The helicopters were called back to their launchpads. The police cruisers went back to their business. Patrick still had the Coke in his hand when the policeman let him out of his car.

The newspaper article's headline read "Reporter finds boy and story." Patrick had wandered safely down several streets, along an abandoned railway, and into the house of a friendly family. I knew Patrick was in God's hands, but I also knew that the story could have turned out very differently. I might never have seen Patrick alive again. This very plausible possibility filled me with a fear I had never before known. I was almost too frightened to cry until he was safely in my arms, safe again from the world.

Patrick's doctor had placed him on a diet that was very low in sugar and carbohydrates, two things that he craves and would live on if he could. I knew that the cravings for these foods were strong and was not at all surprised that he would have gone so far in search of what he craved most. The problem was that Patrick had gone beyond his fence. He had destroyed the boundaries the fence had given him, and with the loss of boundaries went his freedom. I put him in the backyard to see how he got out and if he would try it again, and sure enough he didn't waste any time. He went to the locked wooden gate and pushed against the corner with all his might, making a crack just big enough for him to squeeze through. My heart sank. Now he would have to stay in the house until we could fix the gate to contain him once again.

I thought of the many times I have tried to cross the boundaries of freedom. There always seemed to be something on the other side luring me—some craving or desire that was so strong that I could almost justify stepping outside the truth to satisfy that hunger. I could hear God telling me that if what I desired was good for me, it would be contained inside the beautiful walls He has established. He has given me rules and guidelines to live my life in freedom, free from the danger that waits outside His truth.

Patrick was given freedom with a fence, and then that freedom was taken from him in one action. He found a way to get to what he wanted, but at what a cost! Patrick had no idea what he was giving up that day. He had no idea of the danger that awaited him. With the help of a friend, the gate was secured in a few days, and Patrick was back in the yard on the swing, free again.

All went well with the fence until a few years later, when Patrick figured out how to climb beyond its limits. It was a six-foot, shadowbox, wooden fence, with only a few inches between the slats of wood. Patrick figured out how to put his foot sideways into the opening and climb on the cross slats until he reached the top. Then he merely swung over and dropped to the other side. One quick dip in the neighbor's pool was all he wanted, but in the process, he lost his freedom again. This time it was a week before we could improve the fence.

God once again showed us the beauty of our parish family, when six men came over the very next weekend and spent an entire day putting thin slats of wood over the openings so that Patrick would not have anywhere to put his feet. What once had been a ladder was now a solid wall. The men screwed 336 openings with 336 one-by-six-inch pieces. (Mark counted.) Again, Patrick was free to run in his backyard and swing. The pool never went away. It was always there tempting him, but we just kept making the fence bigger and stronger to keep our little one, who was not so little anymore, inside.

The world pulls hard. It pulls at me, as pools pull at Patrick, but the loving, fatherly hand of God is always there, keeping a strong, secure wall around me. His wall of truth keeps me free.

[B]ut whoever causes one of these little ones
who believe in me to sin, it would be better for him to have
a great millstone fastened round his neck and
to be drowned in the depth of the sea.

—*Matthew 18:6*

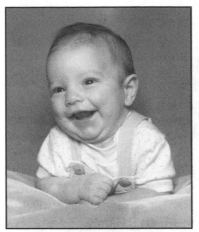 

Patrick at eight weeks old   Patrick at four years old

Getting into the cabinets

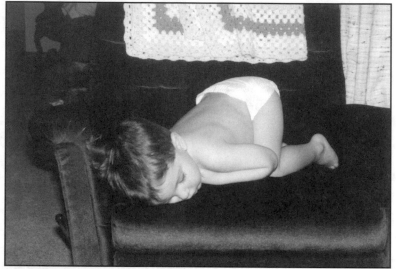

Patrick in perfect comfort

Patrick eating popcorn

In the backyard

Patrick with his brothers and sisters at the pumpkin patch

Christmas morning

Family photo (1998)

Brendan, Kate, Megan, Laura with Bridget, Patrick, Michael, Sean

With something new to wear

Patrick at eight years old

Standing on a deck railing

Patrick and his toys at the table

At the Silvercrest Children's Development Center

On the swing at Silvercrest

Eleventh birthday, Silvercrest

Playing with shaving cream   Patrick upset

Mark and Patrick at the zoo

Mark and Patrick

Beth with Patrick

CHAPTER ELEVEN

My Own Calvary

June 16, 2000

My dear Patrick,

Your brothers and sisters keep asking when you will be home. We all miss you and cannot wait for your summer break. Summer is so strange without you here. You are such an important part of our home. We miss many things about you: your joy and laughter as Sean throws you to the floor for a tickling match, your tears as you come running into the house for a kiss when you've been hurt, and even your endless messes. All are things we miss dearly.

One who I'm sure misses you in her own special way is our adopted, big black lab, Velvet. She thinks she belongs to us, and especially to you. Day and night she sits by the front door. I think she is waiting for you to come home. Even though you are allergic to dogs, Velvet does not seem to bother you, and she takes it upon herself to watch over and protect you. Do you remember the Holy Thursday night when Daddy, Sean, and Laura were at Mass, and you went down to the creek in the dark? It was such a dark night. Brendan and Megan were out with flashlights looking for you, but it was Velvet who found you in the creek covered in mud.

With all the rain we've had recently, the creek is very full, and from the back door I can hear the small waterfall in the creek behind the house. How many hours you've spent behind our house playing on the rocks and splashing in the creek. Just about every day, Daddy carried into the house a handful of muddy clothes that you had left down at the creek. The muddy laundry ended for the most part the day you left. (Michael still contributes his share, however.)

I have always loved washing your clothes and folding them, offering a prayer for you with each little shirt or pair of jeans. I miss you so much. God bless you, my little one.

I love you,
Mommy

We know that in everything God works for good with those who love him, who are called according to his purpose.

—Romans 8:28

aundry has long been a very big part of my everyday life. It is not unusual to do ten loads a day. Some days we may have only five or six, but most days we have around ten loads to wash. There was a time when the number of loads was even higher. Those were the days of potty training two children at once. Patrick and Brendan were in cloth training pants, and Megan and Michael were in cloth diapers. I also used washcloths as baby wipes. So most of the time, I filled all four of my clotheslines with diapers, wipes, and training pants. It was quite a sight. For many years one of my main goals each day was to get all the laundry done. It was always at the top of my things-to-do list. I would gaze upon the piles of freshly folded laundry and think, "I'm getting there." As you can imagine, finding clean, folded laundry on the floor of a closet, under a bed, or—worst of all—in the bottom of the clothes hamper, under very dirty clothes, has been a source of great frustration for me, as it is for most mothers.

Another struggle has been seeing Patrick in his sixth or seventh outfit of the day. Why he continually changes clothes is a mystery, but he loves to try on just about all he owns. After we moved to the country, Patrick frequently would leave his dirty clothes by the creek in our backyard and then just come in and find a new outfit to wear. Sometimes I wouldn't see an outfit for weeks, but then someone would find it, and I would have to wash it a few times before I could recognize it. Patrick's skin is very sensitive to touch, and we spent many years just trying to get him to keep any clothing on at all. Now he keeps it on for short periods of time, but the minute it gets wet or begins to irritate him in any way, he strips it off.

My laundry pile continues to grow, but one day God helped me to let go of the frustration and actually learn to love the laundry. If more is better, then Patrick has definitely made it better.

Let me explain. I was reading about the life of Saint Louis de Montfort. Once, after preaching a very successful mission, he felt the Lord calling him to build a life-sized calvary in thanksgiving for the mission. It was built on a hill in France, and it was beautiful. People came from all over to help. The workers carved life-sized statues, which were used to show the Way of the Cross. Special trees were brought in and planted to represent the beads of the Rosary. People even came from other countries to help Saint Louis build this calvary for God.

Once it was completed, everyone eagerly awaited the coming of the bishop to bless this site of prayer and devotion. It was to be a glorious celebration. The bishop sent word the day before the blessing, however, that the shrine could not be blessed. Saint Louis, seeking an explanation, walked through the night to the bishop's home, and arrived at six in the morning. He found out that the shrine would not be blessed and later learned that all of the work was to be destroyed. Enemies of Saint Louis had lied to the king, telling him that the calvary could be used as a fortress for an invading English army.

Saint Louis accepted the bishop's decree with peace in his heart. He had built it out of obedience to God, and now he would dismantle it out of obedience. He did not allow himself or any of his companions to speak badly about the bishop or the king. He offered up to God all the pain of seeing his calvary dismantled. God accepted his offering, and years later, people from the surrounding area rebuilt it even more beautifully than before.

I began to reflect on the story and what Saint Louis had done. Through this story, the Lord showed me how I could look at my neatly stacked piles of laundry as my own calvary, my own monument of thanksgiving for the children that He had given me. I had to learn that the only reason to do laundry was to honor and glorify God. If I was doing it just to get it done, then I was probably doing it for my own honor and glory. If I was doing it to impress my friends with my efficiency, then I was doing it for the wrong reason. Now all I had to do was to put this lesson into practice. Would I be just as willing to let my calvary of laundry be torn down? God was ready to test me, and He knew just the little guy to call upon to help Him.

As I stood there looking at the last five loads to wash for the day, my thoughts were on which load to do next. I had learned from Saint Louis that I was doing the laundry for God. Just then, someone came running down the stairs to let me know that Patrick had covered the boys' room in toothpaste, something he played with often. The bedspread, sheets, and walls were covered with his artwork. I decided that the bedspread would go in next and then the sheets. "That's easy. No big deal," I thought to myself. Actually, I was quite relieved it was merely toothpaste, because we have had much worse. If you've ever tried to clean Desitin off walls and furniture, you know what I mean.

At that point, I went back to Patrick's room to see if he still had the tube of toothpaste, but he was nowhere to be found. I did, however, notice that he had wet his bed, and that I would need to strip it. It was never just the sheets. He has a way of soaking everything near him, including the mattress cover and some stray articles of clothing. "I guess this is the next load going in," I thought to myself. As I began to strip the sheets, I heard my daughter Laura scream, "Patrick is coming in the back door, and he is covered in mud!" Patrick does not just play in mud; he swims in it, eats it, and experiences it completely. It had been pouring rain for days, so this was first-class mud and a first-class mess.

I had learned many years earlier that little disasters could happen around our house, and so I had trained the other children in the fine art of damage control. Laura had done all she could to stop him in his tracks until reinforcements (that would be me) could arrive. I reached for the pile of clean towels on the table as I made my way to the back door.

Slowly, I peeled off the muddy clothes and used the clean towels to keep the mud from spreading to the carpet and the kitchen. I then carried Patrick to the tub for a bath and left him to soak while I returned to the back door to clean up the mess. "I guess the load of muddy things will have to go in next," I thought to myself, almost laughing at the chain of events that had just taken place. I looked at the four muddy towels on the floor and thought about how they had just come out of the dryer an hour ago. I knew in my heart that I was not taking steps backward. If I washed them for God once, I could wash them again.

My thoughts were interrupted by the all-too-familiar scream of Megan: "Mommy! Patrick's bathtub is overflowing, and the water has soaked the carpet in his room!" I immediately realized that I had forgotten to turn off the special valve to his bathtub that we had installed. (That was a definite no-no.) I grabbed the few remaining clean towels on the table—all that was left of my beautiful calvary—and headed for the bathroom. It was not easy to keep smiling, but with the grace of God and the example of Saint Louis, I was able to make it through.

I had thought that I was in control. I thought that the laundry was going to get done, and that I could rejoice in a job well done. I was reminded, however, that God is always in control. Like Saint Louis de Montfort, I have to be willing for the calvaries I build to be torn down, even if it makes no sense to me. I do the laundry because it is what God is calling me to do at that time, and for no other reason. In that way, all of my work can be an act of sanctification, an offering to God. Yes, God is in control. I'll do it His way.

Great are the works of the LORD,
studied by all who have pleasure in them.

—Psalm 111:2

CHAPTER TWELVE

The Body of Christ

June 22, 2000

My dear Patrick,

Tomorrow Daddy will be at school to pick you up for summer vacation. We are all so excited. Your brothers and sisters are making all sorts of plans for things we can do together when you get home. Right now they are trying to decide who gets to take care of you first. Just like Mommy, everyone wants to be close to you.

The day after you get home, Daddy and Sean will be leaving to go to Tijuana, Mexico, to work in your great uncle Father John's mission. Many people from our church, Saint John's, and our old parish, Our Lady of Mount Carmel, will be going with Daddy and Sean, as they have been for many years. Daddy was very sad that the mission trip is at the same time as your visit home, but he knows it's God's will. He will be gone for only part of your vacation. I think they will actually be building a house for someone in a very poor neighborhood in the city. It is beautiful to see the Mystical Body of Christ at work in the way we care for each other.

Sean usually spends a great deal of time with you, and I know it will be hard not to have him here. Your cousin Joey is planning to help take care of you by taking you swimming often, and we all know how much you will love that. I truly believe that you will do more for Joey than he will do for you. I have seen, day by day, how much God continually blesses those who are a part of your life. Your life is a gift to us. God bless you, my little one.

I love you,
Mommy

For as in one body we have many members,
and all the members do not have the same function,
so we, though many, are one body in Christ,
and individually members one of another.

—Romans 12:4-5

A police car pulled up at our neighbor's house, and I knew our house would be next. For the first time, my children heard me say, "I don't know what to do." I started to cry. I simply didn't know what to do next. Patrick had gotten into the neighbor's pool again. Even though it had been months since he had been over there, they called the police. Short of bringing over information on a twenty-thousand-dollar alarm system, they refused to talk to us about Patrick and the pool. Alarms would not be of much help with Patrick. We usually knew when he was missing. He is just so fast that we didn't know where he went: the street, the pool, the pond, or someone's kitchen. All four were likely candidates.

The neighbors with the pool let us know that it was our responsibility to keep Patrick confined. We weren't allowed to call them if Patrick was missing to see if he was in their yard. They called the police each time he stepped on their property. It was nearly impossible to watch Patrick at all times. Mark's dad once commented, "You can watch Patrick 100 percent of the time, and that's not enough." God knew that we couldn't do it alone. He had given us the Mystical Body of Christ. By the time he got in their pool again, many of our friends from church were already making our home a safer place for Patrick.

It began one very cold winter morning when I woke up and found Patrick outside in the snow. He had opened the kitchen window and pushed out the screen and climbed through. There was no way he could have gotten back into the house since it was locked tight, and a vision of finding my little one frozen in the snow raced through my head. I didn't know how long he had been out there, only that God had awakened me and saved his life. I brought him in, and in no time he was warm and bouncing through the house. I did not bounce back so easily.

Patrick shared a room with his brothers, and there was no way to confine him to the room. Everything we had tried failed, or worked for a short while until Patrick figured out a way to outsmart us. It didn't matter what we tried. We had doctors show us ways to tether him to his bed, but he would soon break the tether. We had considered barriers, but he would simply climb over, around, or through whatever Mark or I could conceive. We knew we couldn't put a dead bolt on the bedroom door. What could we do?

Usually, our friendly next-door neighbors were the first to find out that our latest plan didn't work. Tom and Lisa, Tom and Cindy, Caesar and Jane, and Doug and Cindy had all been great with Patrick. They had some idea of how difficult it was to keep up with this Houdini. Almost everyone around us went out of his way to help with Patrick. It was not unusual to have a neighbor climb on the roof to bring Patrick down after he had gone out a window. Others would bring him back in the wee hours of the morning after he figured out how to stack up chairs and open the lock at the top of the door. They never gave the impression that they were ever put out, only happy they could help.

We went to bed at night never knowing what might awaken us. Once we awoke at about four in the morning to a loud crash of glass breaking. We knew it was either Patrick up to one of his tricks or someone breaking in. We looked in his room, and naturally, he was gone. We went into the kitchen just as Patrick was about to jump off the counter into a sea of glass. He had filled the coffee pot with water and then dropped it on the floor. It was not unusual to find him lying on the bottom of a full tub of water or chewing on the battery from a flashlight. Patrick had developed into a nocturnal creature whose owl-like habits kept us up many nights.

On the day I found him in the snow, we knew we would have to make some major changes in our house or find a new one. We did not have the money to buy a new house in the area, so we knew we would have to make the house we had work. We had no extra money to make changes. Patrick's treatments were not covered by insurance, and the debts just kept increasing. We believed it was our responsibility to provide for Patrick and that we could do it somehow. The harder we tried to cut corners and spend less, the greater the debt grew. Mark was working as many hours as he could, often spending twelve-hour days painting in the summer and on weekends throughout the school year. All of these plans for living within our means and ways to get out of debt blew up in front of us. I could see that God was pushing us to the end. He wanted us to let go, and as long as there was some possibility that we could take care of things on our own, He knew our pride would stay in the way.

After many tears and prayers, God told us that through His Mystical Body, He would protect and care for this special little boy. During this time, He taught me much about humility and swallowing my pride. It was perhaps even more difficult for Mark. Being the husband and father, he wanted so very much to provide all that his family needed. In the case of Patrick, that meant lots of special treatments and medicine that insurance companies often deemed experimental. Mark is a very proud man, and it hurt him deeply to ask anyone for assistance. He would always rather do something the hard way than ask for help. It didn't matter if he was trying to carry furniture, paint a house, fix the car, or deal with Patrick. Mark had learned, somehow, that it was a sign of weakness to ask someone else for assistance. Over the years, however, God had begun to show Mark through Patrick's difficulties that he couldn't do it all alone.

I called a friend, Amy, whose husband, Tom, is a builder, and from there God took over. We went back and forth with the plans, how it would be funded, what loans we could get, and how the parish could help. It was all very hard to accept. So much of our life was laid out for others to analyze and pass judgment on. In the end, kindness, compassion, and generosity overshadowed it all, and by spring ground was broken to begin building an addition onto the back of our house. It was built at a fraction of the cost because friends from the parish did much of the work. It touched my heart deeply to see executives, accountants, engineers, college students, and many others all working together to help frame the rooms.

Some of them weren't even sure how to hammer a nail, but what they did was much more than build a few rooms on to our home. They taught Mark and me and our children what it means to be part of the Body of Christ.

Little by little, the addition began to take shape. It consisted of a very small bedroom, bath, and a large playroom for Patrick. The existing French doors made it possible to see into the addition. Anytime day or night, we could confine Patrick there and know he was safe. The playroom was like a family room where everyone could be together, and Patrick did not have to feel as if he were being punished or put away.

We had taken down part of the fence to allow trucks to enter the backyard with building materials. While the fence was displaced, Patrick slipped past us and off to the pool. I called my friend Amy to be with me when the police arrived. She was in the middle of fixing dinner, but she left everything and came right over. She helped me to see that everyone was doing the best he could for Patrick and that the police would understand. We lived in fear of Patrick being taken from us, and each time the police came, the reality of that possibility ripped through my heart. By the time the police arrived at our door, Mark was home, and my friend had gone.

The officer was very kind and understanding. He told us that he could see all that was being done for Patrick, and he was sorry he had to bother us. The police had come before, and each time they talked to us and came to the same conclusion. We had made so many changes to our home, to our family, and to our way of living, all in an attempt to help Patrick.

By summer, Patrick was safely in his new room. Then we began to work on the rest of the house. We built cabinets in the dining room so we could lock up all the food. The living room was converted to a bedroom for Mark and me so we could be closer to Patrick in case he needed us during the night. Then we put a dead bolt on every door in the house, all fit to one key, and locks on all the windows, fit to another key. Like wardens in a prison, we carried the keys with us at all times and hid the spares, because Patrick learned very quickly that keys opened up the world to him.

God used Patrick once again to teach me the beauty of His Mystical Body, to let me know that Patrick is not only a part of our family but also part of a Church that is working hard to build the Kingdom of God. In coming together to serve Patrick, members of the Church came together to serve Christ.

Whoever humbles himself like this child,
he is the greatest in the kingdom of heaven.

—Matthew 18:4

CHAPTER THIRTEEN

God's Interior Decorator

June 30, 2000

My dear Patrick,

You've been home for such a short time and already your presence has filled our home with a joy that only you can bring. The day you came home, you bounced in the door so happily, with the biggest smile I have ever seen. When our eyes met, you spoke deeply to my heart. You knew you were home with your mommy. I wrapped you in my arms and did not want to let go. You had other plans, as usual.

Your brothers and sisters came running, and though you smiled through it all, I know all the commotion and hugs must have been hard on you. You sat together with them on the sofa with smiles all around. The expression on your face was one of such great joy.

After a quick run through the house to check all the rooms, you yelled "Fing!" and out the front door you went, down the hill, and onto the tree swing, with all the kids trying to keep up with you. From the swing you went to the garden, and from the garden back into the house, saying, "Fi! Fi!" We all knew you wanted a bath, and into the tub you went.

In the few days you've been home, you have reminded us that green craft paint left on the counter in the bathroom is an invitation for you to express your creative decorating skills, that peanut butter and brown sugar leave wonderful tracks through the house, that wallpaper is for peeling, and that it doesn't take long to fill the tub to overflowing. Basically, you've reminded us of your one-of-a-kind, Patrick messes. With God's grace and constant prayer, I'm loving every minute of it. I'm so happy you are home. God bless you, my little one.

I love you,
Mommy

Therefore do not be anxious about tomorrow,
for tomorrow will be anxious for itself.
Let the day's own trouble be sufficient for the day.

—*Matthew 6:34*

*M*y husband, Mark, felt called to return to his hometown of Loogootee, Indiana, to teach high school English and journalism. We resisted the move for a long time, as we were very happy with our parish, our neighborhood, and our home. Through a great deal of prayer, however, Mark finally discerned that he was supposed to accept the offer of a new job. This left us with a very real problem. Our house was not the most desirable for the upscale Carmel market.

Mark accepted the new position and temporarily moved in with his parents at the beginning of the new school year. I was left two and one-half hours away to sell the house on my own—at least, that is what I thought. God and Patrick had it all worked out, and I soon learned it was my job to try to keep up with their plans. We knew selling the house would be difficult because we had tried before. The house was previously on the market for nearly a year, but no one was interested. This time we had even more reason to be concerned because we had made so many changes to the house to accommodate Patrick. We knew it would take a special family with a special need even to show interest.

With all the changes to the house, the building of the addition and the placing of locks on everything, the girls now slept in the master bedroom and chose Pepto Bismol pink for the color of the walls. I had spent hours stenciling flowers around the wall just below the ceiling and cringed at the thought of painting over all of it. We also converted the small hallway between the master bedroom and the upstairs bathroom into a closet on the bedroom side and shelves for storage on the bathroom side. The bathroom part was finished, but the closet was not. It would have required a great deal of work to convert it back to a hallway, but we left that open as an option if the buyer wanted it that way.

Over and over again, I told myself that God would be the one to sell the house and that He had a special family that needed a house like ours. We didn't want to convert anything back until we knew the desires of the people who would buy the house. A wonderful real estate agent took the challenge of helping us. Together, with the help of friends (especially the Franzen family, who helped clean the house from top to bottom), we got the house ready to sell. The real challenge was keeping it that way.

Patrick had learned how to write his name (P-A-T) at school, and he took great joy in going about the house with pens engraving Ts on all the walls. When Mark came home on weekends, one of his jobs was repairing drywall and painting over the Ts all over the house. The other big problem was the carpet. When Patrick took baths, the water rarely stayed in the tub. When Patrick ate dinner, the food rarely stayed on the plate. When Patrick played outside, he often brought a lot of the great outdoors inside. So we had to try to keep the carpet clean. We had long ago given up on commercial products. Patrick was more challenging than that. Our carpet cleaner, Rick, was always on call to get something out of the carpet before someone came to look at the house. Patrick's love for staining the carpet really challenged Rick, but he never complained. He just showed up when I called. Patrick's messes required professional help.

The weeks turned into months, and very few people came to look at the house. Carol, our real estate agent, assured me that it was just a slow time of the year, and she did everything she could to attract a buyer. I did not realize it at the time, but I was still clinging to the notion that the sale of the house depended on my ability to keep up with Patrick's creative redecorating. I knew that God would be the one to sell the house, but I just couldn't let go of my sense of control. "Do I know in my heart that God will be the one Who sells the house?" I asked myself—because often my actions didn't show it.

God opened my eyes one fall morning in October after the house had been on the market for four months. Everyone was rushing about trying to get out the door for school, and I was in the family room nursing the baby, when the phone rang. It was the real estate agent wanting to bring someone over to see the house at ten that morning. I looked around, said a quick prayer, swallowed hard, and said, "Sure." Cleaning up from breakfast alone would take at least an hour. As I hung up the phone, all the things I needed to do to ensure the house would sell ran through my head. I began to panic, so God used my little Patrick to take drastic means and take the reins away from me once again.

One of the children yelled, "Mom, come quick! You won't believe what Patrick did!" This was not an uncommon statement in our home. As always, I made my way through the house to the stairway from which the loud shrieking voice had come, and there it was: a big hole right through the wallpaper and the drywall. The children were more than happy to explain, all at the same time, how Patrick had been lying there tapping his foot on the wall and then suddenly kicked it really hard, and his foot went right through. Patrick just lay there gazing at the wall with a look of peace and satisfaction that comes from a job well done. It's a look you might see in someone who just accomplished a great feat.

All I could do at that moment was smile. For I knew for certain, in my heart, that only God could sell the house, and the words that came to my lips confirmed it. The children stood there looking at me, waiting for my reaction. You can imagine their relief when they heard me say with a smile, "God sure has a funny way of selling houses. I don't think I would put a hole in the wall just before a showing."

In a calm and peaceful, yet hurried way, I got the older children and Patrick off to school. Suddenly, while looking at the hole, and knowing I was a dangerous person with drywall, I thought of a friend, Mike. I called, and he just happened to be home from work that day and would have no trouble repairing the wall that morning. By ten, the house was clean and the wall repaired, including the wallpaper.

Despite all these efforts, there was no sale. No problem.

See that you do not despise one of these little ones;
for I tell you that in heaven their angels always behold the face
of my Father who is in heaven.

—Matthew 18:10-11

CHAPTER FOURTEEN

In the Father's Arms

July 5, 2000

My dear Patrick,

Today, we drove to Evansville for a family picture for the church directory. Getting everyone ready for the picture has always been easier than keeping you still long enough for the photographer to take it. Today, you surprised us. Daddy always has to disguise the fact that he is holding on to you with all his strength. Today, for the first time, he didn't have to hold on at all. You sat beautifully. Your only concern during the photo session was that your shoe was untied, and that's understandable. Once it was tied, I could see that you were trying very hard to do what you were told, even though it probably made very little sense to you to sit still and smile for the camera.

It is almost time for you to return to school from summer vacation, and my heart is breaking. I lie awake at night crying and wondering how you will handle going back to school. I wish there were some way I could explain it to you, so that you could understand and not feel as if we don't want you at home. When I try to talk to you about it, you just smile and turn away or look off into a world of your own.

I know how much you have loved being here. Now that Sean and Daddy are back from Mexico, our entire family is once again together here in our home. In the past months, while you've been gone, Daddy has said many times, "I want to go get Patrick. I want to bring him home." It has been very hard for him to have you away. Yet God has given us all the strength to accept His will and trust in Him. I will cherish these few days we have left with you here. God bless you, my little one.

I love you,
Mommy

Humble yourselves therefore under the mighty hand of God, that in due time he may exalt you.

—*1 Peter 5:6*

It was five o'clock on Sunday morning, and there I was on the phone with the poor doctor who was unlucky enough to be on call that day. Patrick had never wheezed in his life, but during the night he had woken up with a very audible wheeze. "He's dancing around the living room and watching *Chitty Chitty Bang Bang*," I tried to explain. "But is he in any kind of distress?" she asked for the third time. "Well, with each breath his sternum is pulling in and his ribs are flaring out, but other than that, it is just the wheezing," I said rather calmly. "Get him to the emergency room," was her only response. As I hung up the phone I thought, "He isn't going to like this." I prayed, "Lord, help us through this, especially Patrick."

As I expected, Patrick did not respond well to the emergency room. The bright lights and the noise must have been extremely painful for him. I'm sure the whole thing made no sense to him, especially when it came time for a respiratory treatment. The therapist tried over and over to put the mask gently near his face. I could see by his reaction that he would not have anything to do with it. He must have been thinking, "I am struggling for air, and she wants to cover up my face with this mask full of smoke. I don't think so." He proceeded to fight us with every ounce of energy he had. This only made it harder for him to breathe, and eventually I had to put a stop to the therapist's effort.

After letting Patrick calm down for a minute, I said, "Either we hold him down and put the mask on his face, or else we take it away, because he knows that as long as he can fight us, he will. Once he knows he can't move, he will calm down." She reluctantly agreed, then said, "I just don't want to upset him. He's already struggling so hard to breathe." Once I had Patrick held down firmly, the treatment went very smoothly. He just rested in my arms.

A few hours later, Patrick's condition improved, and he was released from the hospital. We thought we were done with the emergency room for one day, but we were wrong. During the second trip to the emergency room that day, the doctor could not understand why I hadn't given Patrick his medicine the way he had instructed. Patrick does not like to take liquid medication, and he could detect a drop in a gallon of orange juice. When I tried to explain how Patrick spit it across the room and how hard it was to hold him down, the doctor's response was, "I'll have my nurse show you how to do it." At that he turned and left the room. I prepared myself for what promised to be a very interesting demonstration. By the time it was over, it took four nurses to show me how to give the medication, and none of them wanted to come home with me so we could do it again.

How often God has had to pin me down in order to give me the medication or the treatment I have needed. While Patrick was fighting a battle with viral-induced bronchial asthma, I felt the Lord teaching me about His love, and that submission to His love can only bring good. When we fight against His loving will, we are only hurting ourselves. Patrick's constant example has taught me much. God always gives me a chance to learn a good lesson when I need one.

I was like a little girl fighting with another child over a toy. The little girl eventually pulls hard enough for the other child to let go. Both the girl and the toy then fly across the room. Now she has her precious toy, but she is too sore to play with it.

I did not want a toy, but I did want the chicken pox—not for myself, but for my two youngest children, Kate, who was three, and Bridget, who was one. The older kids were in school, and I didn't have a newborn in the house. I knew this was the perfect time for the chicken pox, and I had been waiting for someone we knew to say those wonderful words, "So-and-so has the chicken pox."

The words came from one of Mark's cousins, who said, as I greeted her after Mass, "I have to go. My son is home sick with the chicken pox." Needless to say, I was elated, and Mark could tell by the look on my face what I had in mind. He said, "No!"—to which I quickly responded, "It would be perfect." Shaking his head, Mark said, "Mom and Dad are waiting to meet us after Mass for dinner, and you have too much going on right now with me living down here and with you trying to sell the house. I just don't think we should do it." I thought he just didn't understand how important it was for them to get the chicken pox while still young (yet not too young), or they could get them again. I continued trying to make plans with his cousin for us to stop by on our way to dinner with the family or to call her if we weren't coming. Like the child pulling for the toy, I continued to pull, and after awhile Mark reluctantly agreed, "If you are sure you want to do this . . ." I was very sure. I had done it before, and it had worked like a charm.

All went as planned, and, as usual, I got what I wanted. When we returned home Sunday night, I quickly went to the calendar to mark the date that my two beautiful little girls would break out and be covered in red spots. My heart sank as I looked at the little box there on the calendar. There was no room to write chicken pox in the box because there in big bold letters I had already written "Family Pictures." I didn't know whether to laugh or cry. I had waited two years to have this picture taken, and I had hoped to have them back in time for Christmas. Now my stubbornness may have ruined everything. If I had listened to Mark's request to keep the girls away from his cousin's son, I wouldn't be facing such a problem. I prayed, "Dear Lord, let the weeks of waiting and wondering be enough. Please don't let them get the chicken pox." On the day of the pictures, my prayer was answered. The children had beautiful little faces. They never did get the chicken pox, but I learned a wonderful lesson that God had been gently using Patrick to teach me for years. God knows that when the gentle approach doesn't work, I, like Patrick, need to be held firmly in His arms to receive the medicine I so desperately need.

Lo, sons are a heritage from the LORD,
the fruit of the womb a reward.
Like arrows in the hand of a warrior
are the sons of one's youth.
Happy is the man who has his quiver full of them!
He shall not be put to shame
when he speaks with his enemies in the gate.

—*Psalm 127:3-5*

CHAPTER FIFTEEN

A Place for Us

July 9, 2000

My dear Patrick,

We knew this day had to come. It's late, and everyone is asleep. I can't stop crying. You were so happy when Daddy told you it was time to get in the car. With Kate and Bridget crying, "Daddy, please don't take our Patrick away," you headed for the door. You have always loved going for rides with Daddy. No matter how many times we tried to explain, you showed no signs of understanding. Daddy and Sean were taking you back to school, and you didn't know until you woke up in the car and recognized where you were. Daddy told me how much you cried. I knew you would.

I did not have the strength to go back to school with you. I didn't even have the strength to help Laura take care of your younger brothers and sisters. All I could do was go into my room and cry. I ate almost an entire box of chocolates that my sister Mary had sent Daddy and me for our anniversary. I don't know why I thought it would make me feel better, because it didn't.

What did help was praying and seeing God's hand in your life. I thought about how God brought Daddy and me together on a retreat for young adults and how we knew from the start that we would marry and strive to make God the center of our lives. I thought about how He has always provided the perfect home for you even though it takes awhile for us to see it. In prayer, God assured me that He has something very special planned for you and that this is all part of His plan. I know God will take good care of you, and I try to trust in His ways, but the tears keep coming. When you are home, I constantly ask where you are and what you are doing. When you are away from us at school, however, I constantly wonder how you are, if you are lonely, scared, or hungry. As always, I will ask God to watch over and bless you, my little one.

I love you,
Mommy

———— ❖ ————

The LORD *will keep your going out and your coming in from this time forth and for evermore.*

—Psalm 121:8

"It sure would be a lot easier to sell that house if you didn't have Patrick making so many messes." As these words came to my ears, I was tempted to agree, but my heart said, "No." Patrick and everything about him, including his ability to dismantle the house, was important in God's plan. The speaker meant to be sympathetic, but to me, the words were a rejection of my son. Was God using Patrick's messes to keep the house from selling? I thought, "Maybe our new house isn't ready for us yet." I was sure of one thing: All the messes he made, especially with water, could not possibly help sell the house. I would just accept the messes and wait.

While we waited for the house to sell, we combed Loogootee and the surrounding area looking for a house that would work for our family. We could not find anything that would work for Patrick. It was hard to find a house in Loogootee that was far from highways, ponds, and railroad tracks, but we kept looking. Someone who knew of our search suggested in all kindness that we just teach Patrick to stay off the street. After years of holding Patrick's hand tightly to keep him from running toward cars, I knew he would not live long enough to learn. If we lived near a busy road, our house would be a prison, not just for Patrick, but for all our children. Every bit of maternal instinct in me said, "No!" No matter how perfect the house might be otherwise, we just couldn't live on a highway. That narrowed our search considerably. The real estate agent we were working with just didn't seem to understand our concerns and kept showing us houses on busy streets and state highways.

One weekend while we were house hunting, some friends Mark had met at church invited us to a cookout at their home in a beautiful subdivision just outside town. When I looked outside the back door of their house, the view took my breath away. When I could breathe again, I said, "All I want is a house with this view." I was only kidding, but little did I know that one day God would give me such a house.

Later, I pointed out to the children exactly which colors I wanted our new house to be painted. (Being married to a painter has its advantages.) I told them I wanted beige with white trim and forest green shutters. Mark wasn't with us at the time, and I never mentioned it to him. I knew the last thing he needed to hear was that he would be doing more painting as soon as we found a suitable house.

Mark only wanted a house that would work for Patrick. We kept hearing comments from friends and family like "It would be a lot easier to find a house for the family if you didn't have to think of Patrick's needs." We both knew that the house that fit Patrick's needs would be the best for our entire family. We just had to wait for God's time to show us that house.

Then, one crazy morning, while I was racing against the clock as usual, I was at a meeting with my three youngest children, Michael, Kate, and Bridget. I called Patrick's school, Westfield Elementary, to see if the staff there were able to get the stool specimen we needed from him, and they told me they had it. Even while we were trying to sell the house and hold things together while Mark was working in another town, we still had Patrick's medical concerns to consider. He had been having chronic stomach pains and cramping. The doctors wanted to see if they could determine the reasons before we treated him with Secretin, a new drug used for autistic patients. I had to get the sample to the hospital right away, since they were sending their specimens to the lab soon. I had only a short time to pick up the specimen, take it to the hospital, and be at Our Lady of Mount Carmel to pick up Megan from kindergarten. If all went perfectly, I could make it.

So I left the little ones with a friend at the meeting and started out on another mad dash. I zipped over to Patrick's school, picked up the specimen, and drove hurriedly to the hospital. When I arrived at the hospital lab with the specimen, I could not find Patrick's insurance card. I was sure it was in my billfold, and yet it seemed to have disappeared. The receptionist told me that without the insurance card, the specimen could not go out with the next shipment to the main lab. We had tried for days to get this specimen, and if it were not sent that morning, we would have to go through the whole procedure again. She told me that if I could call in the information in the next half hour, they would send it. After all we had gone through to get the specimen, I agreed.

As I drove home, I asked God, "Why are you sending me home to get the insurance information? I have to get to the school. I don't have time for this." I ran through the front door and looked around for the card but couldn't find it. My time was running out. I opened my billfold to get the number for the lab's receptionist, and there, next to the lab card, was Patrick's insurance card. My mind was filled with questions: "Why, Lord? Why did I have to come home? I'm going to be late." I took a deep breath and began to call the lab when the doorbell rang.

It was time for God to use Patrick and his love for covering himself and everything around him in water to sell the house.

A year had passed since the day I had decided to throw away the little plastic pool we had bought for Patrick to use in the summer. After Patrick spent a summer splashing and playing in the water and bringing endless soaking wet clothes through the house, I decided it was time to get rid of the pool. I put it out for the trashmen and hoped that it would be gone before Patrick returned from school. We had nowhere to store it for the winter, and Patrick, no doubt, would fill it in the middle of winter, only to freeze and catch a cold.

It sat there all that day, and just before Patrick came home from school, a woman came to the door and asked if she could have the pool. I said, "Sure," and told her why we were getting rid of it and that it was in good shape. Her name was Mary, and she smiled. With a soft, kind voice, she said, "I want the pool for my son who is autistic." She went on to tell me that they didn't live in the neighborhood, but that she was taking her son to his tutor's house down the street and had spotted the pool. I invited Mary and her children in for a quick visit, and then they left with the pool. Soon after they left, the trashmen came down the street, unusually late, but there is no such thing as a coincidence with God. They were late for a reason. I was supposed to meet Mary, this kind Christian woman.

I did not see this woman again for a year, and then God brought her back into my life. While pulling out of a parking spot at the store, I noticed a woman waving at me. After a few moments I recognized that it was Mary. I hadn't seen her since the day that she took our pool. We talked for a few moments, and I mentioned that we hoped to be moving soon to southern Indiana, and then I said good-bye and left.

I had forgotten all about that chance meeting on the morning I was looking for our insurance card, and now, as I opened the door, there stood Mary and her daughter on my doorstep. She told me that she had extra time after an appointment and that she decided to stop by and see the house because she felt the Lord was telling her and her husband to buy it.

Her words did not register in my head. The house was far from ready to show. There were no fresh-cut flowers in a vase, no muffins just out of the oven. The beds weren't even made, and every door was locked. I had no time to talk, for I still had to call the lab and get to school to pick up Megan. I quickly handed her the key and told her she was welcome to walk through the house while I was on the phone.

She loved it. She told me that all the locks were wonderful and that all the "Jesus crosses" (Patrick's Ts) were adorable. The pink room would be perfect for their daughters, and the closet was best left unfinished, so that she and her husband could finish it the way they wanted. She loved the house just as it was, and all I could do was thank God for Patrick's water messes and Ts on the walls.

Mary and her husband, John, made an offer on the house within the next few days. It fit their family perfectly since their autistic son had many of the same needs that Patrick does. By preparing the house for Patrick, we had also prepared it for their son. Only a family with a special-needs child could fully appreciate all that we had done. The things we were afraid no one would want fit their family's needs perfectly.

Now we had someone to buy our house, but we didn't have a house to move into. One day after school, Mark went over to look at a wooded lot we had looked at many times before. He felt he should go look at it once more, even though we had pretty much ruled out the possibility of building. When he arrived, the word "Sold" was written there on the sign, so he drove past it to the end of the road to turn around. It was a dead-end lane. There in front of him was another sign. This one read "For sale by owner." Mark wondered if another lot were for sale, since there was ample room for building.

He looked up to see a little beige house with white trim and green shutters, up on a hill, looking out over fields and pastures. He looked over the landscape and noticed that from where he was standing, he could see the back of our friends' house where we had been for the cookout. In fact, we had much of the same view. Mark had not seen this house previously, and when he called the owners, they told him that they had just put out the sign and that he could see the house in a few days.

When Mark told me about the house and said that it was miles from any highway or railroad track, I knew it was the house God had planned for us. The location was perfect. The property is about two and a half acres of woods and fields, with pasture in front and a creek in back. The house itself was nothing like the one we had envisioned for Patrick, but we knew that with God's help, we could make it work.

In no time, we had bought the house and begun to renovate it, and the old, moldy carpet was replaced with wood and tile. The walls were covered with scrubbable paint and wallpaper, and we began to make plans to build an addition with a special play area to keep Patrick safe. Yes, God had kept our house from selling until he had the perfect house ready for us. The view still takes my breath away. The valleys and trees painted in the beautiful colors of the four seasons remind me of how God used Patrick to sell our house and buy the perfect home for our family, including Patrick.

Let the children come to me, and do not hinder them;
for to such belongs the kingdom of heaven.

—Matthew 19:14

CHAPTER SIXTEEN

Needs and Wants

July 18, 2000

My dear Patrick,

We have returned from our visit to Uncle Greg and his family in North Carolina. We missed you so much. Daddy and I wanted to be able to take you with us, but we knew the trip would be too hard on you, not to mention extremely dangerous. In the wee hours of the morning, we drove south through New Albany, Indiana, and right past your school. Everyone was asleep in the car except Daddy, and I think that was for the best. Your brothers and sisters would have had a hard time understanding why we didn't stop and pick you up. In silence, Daddy just drove and cried and prayed for you.

You have such a wonderful daddy, who loves you dearly. We all love you dearly, even your little sisters who are the ones who usually get hurt when you get upset. It seems you have been able to teach us in a beautiful (though sometimes painful) way the joy that comes with unconditional love. That is Christ-centered love.

Do you remember the day before you left for school? You were standing alone in the dining room when Sean came up from behind, gave you a big hug, and kissed you on the head. As he turned to walk away, I could see sadness in his face. He loves you so much. I don't think either of you knew I was watching from the other room. I will never forget what I saw.

God has blessed you with very special brothers and sisters. Teachers and therapists have told us many times that one of the greatest helps for you has been that you have so many siblings so close in age. They have been good models for you to try to imitate. There is always someone there to challenge you, to encourage you, to help you.

For many years, your brothers and sisters could not see anything you were doing for them. All they could see was how you destroyed their toys, made endless messes throughout the house, and eventually began to hurt them. Through it all, they continued to love you no matter what. They hardly ever complained. Now, little by little, God is showing them all that you have done for them, and how you are truly a blessing. They want you home. As soon as we returned home from vacation, they began asking when we could see you. I hope it will be soon, because I can't wait to hold you. God bless you, my little one.

I love you,
Mommy

———◆◆◆◆◆———

Do not lay up for yourselves treasures on earth,
where moth and rust consume and where thieves break in
and steal, but lay up for yourselves treasures in heaven,
where neither moth nor rust consumes and
where thieves do not break in and steal.
For where your treasure is, there will your heart be also.

—Matthew 6:19-21

There were times when my children wondered if I was going to make it through another one—not another tornado or raging thunderstorm, but a Saturday morning drive past all the garage sale signs. These people I was passing may have for sale, at a very cheap price, exactly what I needed but didn't know I needed, or something I wanted, but didn't know existed. Garage sales made me want to stop just to make sure that if something were there, I wouldn't be passing up the opportunity to purchase it.

After many years of power garage-sale shopping and trying to make sure I was at the right place at the right time with plenty of cash in hand, I realized that I was always going to be at least one step behind someone else. No matter how fast I ran from one sale to the other, no matter how early I got there, I always heard, "Oh, we sold a lot of those earlier." I often heard, "Someone just bought the only one we had." I finally had to change my plan of action. I decided a simple prayer was in order: "Lord, help me to be able to stop at the sales you want me to, keep me from buying what I don't need, and help me find what I do." A certain peace came over me from then on, a peace that took the power shopper out of me. Oh, I'm still fast, but more in order to save time than in order to get my hands on a treasure before someone else does. I began to see that what I needed would be there when I got there, if the item was something I truly needed and not just wanted.

I've struggled most of my life with wants and needs. As a child, I can remember seeing my mother in the checkout line at the grocery store with what seemed to be a great deal of money in her hands, and I would wonder why she wasn't buying candy. It made no sense to me. The older I got the more I dreamed of being able to buy things I wanted or thought I needed without having to worry about the cost, and yet at the same time I loved the idea of being one of Mother Teresa's Missionaries of Charity. Then I could live in complete service to Christ, owning nothing. It seemed I could only do one or the other, since there was no way to do both. God knew, however, that He wanted me to do just that: He wanted me to buy material things, use them, but not own them. All was to belong only to Him.

It was a widow with six children, living in a small, two-room home in a village in the Andes Mountains, who best prepared me for the life to which God was calling me. One day, word came to the village that an old woman who lived in a shack farther up the mountain had fallen and broken her hip. In no time, four men stopped their work and started up the mountain. It took several hours to reach her, and the men returned with her in a stretcher made of an old blanket and two sticks. One of the men asked, "Where will we take her?" The widow quickly answered, "She will come stay with me. I have plenty of room. She can sleep in my bed, and I will sleep on the floor with the children. We will be able to manage just fine."

When I returned to the United States after that visit to Peru, I could truly see how people with many possessions could be so attached to them that they couldn't give away any of them. Yet a poor widow in Peru was so detached from the little she owned that she gave all she had. I saw people who had closed their lives to another child because their three-bedroom house could not hold another. I wondered if I would ever have so much that I could not give it back to God in the way the widow had done. Over the years, God has given me many chances to give back to Him all that He has given me. As my love for Him has grown, He has helped decrease my delight in material things.

Many times, God has given me something and then asked me to loosen my grip and give it back to Him. Once again, His little helper Patrick is the one who asks for it back. All the pleasure of owning something is multiplied a million-fold when you let go of it. Mark and I decided very early in our parenting years that everything we owned would be subject to alteration at any time, and we were not going to get upset over it. Basically, if it was going to make us upset, it wasn't worth having. God took us at our word and has given us many opportunities to practice our resolution: everything from a can of green paint on the new carpet, to a black pen exploding on the hood of our new (secondhand) white car, to fork holes in our antique dining room table. Mark has even had to replace our toilets frequently because of the objects (plastic elephants and rabbits, or half of a plastic Easter egg) that Patrick feels the need to wedge into them. When even the most skilled plumbers can't open one of Patrick's clogs, we've found it's cheaper to replace the toilet. I no longer worry. Mark repaints our walls about three times a year. It's easier than trying to clean all the pen and pencil marks. So what if something breaks? That stress has been taken from me.

The joy of letting go is one thing I have tried to teach my children, and the beauty of their response has been a great witness to me. Brendan, when he was ten years old, was sitting on the sofa next to Patrick one summer morning. Suddenly, I heard Brendan cry out, "Oh, no!" As I looked, there sat Patrick with scissors and Brendan's Cincinnati Reds' baseball cap. Patrick had made a four-inch cut right up the back of the hat. The hat was very special to Brendan, and he wore it everywhere. After taking the scissors from Patrick, I discussed with Brendan how the hat was a gift from God, and how even the chance to play baseball was a gift from God that Patrick may never know. Brendan looked at Patrick and then at the hat and said, "I can still wear it. It will remind me to pray for Patrick that someday he will get to play baseball." He then put his arm around Patrick and said, "Come on, Patrick. Let's go swing." My little Brendan towered over me as I watched him walk arm in arm outside with Patrick. The joy Patrick gave Brendan that day was worth more than a thousand baseball caps, but what he gave me could only be measured by the tear in my eye.

Truly, I say to you, as you did it to one of the least of these my brethren, you did it to me.

—Matthew 25:40

CHAPTER SEVENTEEN

What Really Matters

August 6, 2000

My dear Patrick,

I'm sorry we can't come to see you this weekend. Everyone is sick, and I don't want you to risk catching whatever it is we have. I want so much to hold you. It is always hard to go for long periods of time without seeing you. You have never even shown us that you have any concept of time, and yet your smiling face and your jumping up and down tell us how much you love seeing us when we come to pick you up.

Grandma and Grandpa miss you, too. They have not been able to make the weekend visits with us to see you, but they call when we get home to see how you are doing. I know how much you love them and miss not seeing them. God blessed you with wonderful grandparents, both Mommy's parents and Daddy's parents. They know what a very special gift you are.

Grandpa Gibbons can't be here with you anymore to chase you around and play with you as he did when you were little, but he will be with you in heaven. Grandpa Matthews will be here, however, when you come home. He is often here working in the garden, always calling to your brothers and sisters to bring buckets or tools. The garden is overflowing this time of year. I can hardly freeze and can all the vegetables quickly enough.

I remember seeing you stand on the big tree stump in the garden last summer, watching Grandpa hoe between the rows of corn and beans. It was soon after that we found out he was very sick with cancer. The doctor had to remove Grandpa's bladder. We never thought we would see him in the garden again, but God knew better. Grandpa just celebrated his eighty-second birthday, and when it comes to gardening, there are few who can keep up with him. I pray you will spend many more days together with your brothers and sisters, helping Grandpa in the garden. We miss you dearly. God bless you, my little one.

I love you,
Mommy

Do not be conformed to this world but be transformed by the renewal of your mind, that you may prove what is the will of God, what is good and acceptable and perfect.

—Romans 12:2

It was destined to be the perfect experience for my children. How did I know? I read about it in a parents' magazine, of course. I noticed the picture and read all about it. For a long time I had wanted to garden with my children, but being a city girl I didn't know too much about gardening. Now, because of a magazine article, I knew everything I needed to know about creating the perfect garden, and I was ready to make it a reality.

I had been sitting in the waiting room at the doctor's office, paging through the magazine, when the picture caught my eye. It was a picture of a little boy and girl, dressed perfectly in pastels and white. It showed them smiling as they placed their toy shovel and rake into the rich, black, perfectly tilled soil. Since I had never gardened with my children before, I didn't know what to expect. Thanks to the magazine, however, I now had a pretty good idea what it would be like. I just needed to take a few simple steps to create this scene for myself and my children.

With the picture of the perfect gardening experience clear in my head, we began to garden. About the only thing that fit the picture was that the sun was shining. In fact, it was beating down on us, and I was hot, sweaty, and covered in dirt. As I looked around at my gardening crew, I saw nothing that resembled the picture in my head. The children were suffering from my determination to make it work, and I did not see smiles on their faces, only dirt. Their clothes were covered in mud, and I doubt even the socks matched. Half of them had abandoned their shoes and were running in and out of the house with dirty little feet. The children in the magazine were beautiful with bright white tennis shoes and matching little outfits. If my children were on the cover of a magazine, it would have to be *Muddy Kids Monthly*. We had been working hard to turn the soil, but no matter what we did, we could not change the hard clay beneath our feet into clumps of rich, black soil. My children somehow survived through another one of my failed attempts to be the perfect mother.

Years have passed since that day, and we now have a very large, beautiful garden, no thanks to me or the magazine. Mark and his father have spent many hours preparing the soil, fertilizing it, and caring for the garden. The children, especially Michael, love to spend time in the garden with their grandpa and daddy. We can always see Michael (usually barefoot) running down the hill to help. With smiles on their faces, Mark and the children bring buckets full of beautiful green beans, red, ripe tomatoes, new potatoes, endless zucchini, and sweet corn into my kitchen all summer. The experience my children have with gardening now far surpasses the one in the magazine. What I saw that day was artificial and fake, created to make me think that happiness comes with what is on the pages of a magazine. What my children have is real.

It has taken me a long time to move away from the images I've seen on television or in magazines. I think they will always be in my head, tempting me to believe that things have to be a certain way—or else, what will people think? Our world is constantly telling us how to build the perfect happy home. Where do the clutter under the bed and the piles of dirty clothes fit in? I get it set in my mind that things need to be a certain way, and it's hard for me to budge.

Once, God spent nearly an entire year trying to get me to budge. On the one hand, I had decided that my home would be neat and orderly, just as I had seen on the cover of so many magazines. On the other hand, Patrick had decided that drawers should not have knobs, and that was that. He proceeded to take the knobs off every dresser, desk, and cabinet in the house. At first it was not so bad, but after awhile, it began to wear on us. It is very hard to open drawers without knobs, and the knobs and screws were always all over the floor. No matter what we did to try to convince him that the knobs didn't need to be off, he insisted that they had to be. Once, I sat with him and made him put every knob back on a dresser. It took almost an hour. Within a few minutes after I had left the room, however, he took every knob off again. I never knew how many knobs you can have in one house, but Patrick knew, and he was determined to keep them off the drawers and cabinets.

As time went on, I began to ask God to help Patrick understand that he didn't need to take the knobs off. In my prayer, I heard God say that Patrick would stop taking the knobs off. Then I heard His voice in my heart, "When will *you* stop?" I was not prepared to hear that. Stop what? Everything I was doing was important and was part of what I needed to do to be a good mother. Then God whispered quietly in my heart, "Homemade bread is good, but if you don't have time to smile, buy the bread at the store. A perfect fall day can include baking an apple pie, but it is not required. Scrub your home with love, and keep your soul in order, and everything else will fall into place."

After many months, Patrick changed his mind and decided that knobs belong on the drawers and cabinets, but his perception of how things need to be is still a little different. It wasn't long until he decided that slices of American cheese belonged on the windows, and they can't have any rips or tears in them or he would throw a fit. Next, he began lining up all his toys in perfect rows. Sometimes, Patrick insists that everyone in the family needs to be wearing hats. That is usually not a problem until he tries to get Daddy to wear a baby bonnet. It's impossible to convince Patrick otherwise. I guess God allows Patrick to help me see that my ways, as important as they may seem to me, are not always God's ways—no matter what the magazine rack displays.

Grandchildren are the crown of the aged,
and the glory of sons is their fathers.

—*Proverbs 17:6*

CHAPTER EIGHTEEN

Speaking in Silence

September 8, 2000

My dear Patrick,

I actually got to hear you on the phone today. When John the staff member said he was going to put you on the phone to talk to me, I didn't think you would do it. You usually get upset when someone hands you the phone. Today I could hear you trying to talk. You may not have understood what you were doing, but it was wonderful to hear some of the familiar sounds you make.

I knew it was you. No one else in the world sounds like you do. God made sure of that when He created you to be one of His unique, special children. It always amazes me how as a mother I can pick out in a crowd not only the sounds you make, but also the voices of all your brothers and sisters. I even know each one of their cries.

Today, I could hear you trying to repeat what John was saying. It was beautiful. Daddy and I long to hear you speak someday, Patrick, but for now we are happy just to hear whatever sounds you can make. We know how hard you struggle with speech.

Sometimes your sweetest words come in your silence. Although you have always liked to jump on my bed in the quiet stillness of the morning, leaving the sheets and blankets in a mess, you still prefer to climb into bed next to me for a hug. Patrick, you can say more to me in one brief moment of silence, looking at me with your beautiful eyes, than words ever will say. I cherish those moments.

For now, I will thank God for the few moments I was able to share with you on the phone. I hope hearing your Mommy's voice brought you some comfort. God bless you, my little one.

I love you,
Mommy

She opens her mouth with wisdom,
and the teaching of kindness is on her tongue.
She looks well to the ways of her household,
and does not eat the bread of idleness.
Her children rise up and call her blessed;
her husband also, and he praises her.

—*Proverbs 31:26-28*

inner needs to be on the table in fifteen minutes. I've just put in twice the amount of Minute Rice that the recipe calls for. I gave the children permission to hand out cookies to the neighborhood, and Patrick has painted himself and my bathroom with that bright pink nail polish that I knew I would never use but just couldn't bring myself to throw away. Has this mother gone crazy? No. You may have guessed it: I'm on the phone. I'm not sure why my ability to function as a mother ceases when I'm on the phone, or what keeps me talking when I can see my home falling apart around me. All I know is that it happens far too frequently. I guess I've always liked to talk too much.

I quickly hung up the phone and raced to the bathroom with Patrick, only to find what I had hoped I wouldn't find. Yes, the bathroom was covered in bright pink. As I quickly put Patrick in the tub, just to keep him in one place, many thoughts raced through my head. "What was I thinking when I bought that color nail polish? What made Patrick decide to dump the entire bottle of nail polish remover, the only thing that would remove the polish, down the drain?" These thoughts and more raced through my head until I stopped in my tracks and asked God, "Is this what it takes to get me off the phone?" I knew the answer to that one was yes. I wondered why. Why did God use Patrick to get me off the phone so often? Was it the neglect of my home, or was I about to offend Him with gossip? Maybe both.

God put in my heart a story of a young girl and her wise old friend who lived in a cottage by the sea. The young girl struggled with the constant need to be talking about something. One day, without thinking, she blurted out something about her friend that was not meant for anyone else to hear. She soon realized what she had done, and even though she tried to stop it, it spread like fire through the town. When she arrived at the cottage, she could see that her friend was in pain and had been crying. She asked what she could do to make it right, and her friend handed her a jar of sea salt and a note. The friend then asked her to go to the shore and pour all the salt from the jar into the sea, then read the note. Quickly, she did as she was told and poured every grain of salt into the sea. She picked up the note, and tears filled her eyes as she read, "When you can collect every grain of salt that you poured into the sea, then you will be able to repair the damage you have done." She knew, as she tasted the salt from her tears, that the salt she put in the ocean was no longer hers to collect. It had been taken away by the waves.

I knew that if I were neglecting my children, or about to hurt anyone in any way by saying something that didn't need to be said, I could only thank God for Patrick and pink nail polish. I also knew that I had a long way to go, and it would be only by His grace that I could resist the temptation not to gossip or talk too much. As I looked at Patrick, sitting there in silence, I felt God leading my heart to pray for the gift of silence—the gift of being able to keep quiet even when I have something important to say or a story to tell, the gift of letting another speak first and then taking a moment to pray before letting words leave my mouth. But most of all, I prayed for the grace to show others how I see Christ in someone, even though that person, like me, is far from perfect.

For more than eleven years now, I have waited to hear Patrick speak, to hear him say, "I love you." Patrick started to say a few words when he was a year old, but by two he lost all that he had learned and could make only rhythmic, high-pitched sounds. It took a very difficult two hours in the office of a speech pathologist with a jar of cookies, reserved only for the "good little boy" at the end of the session, for us to get a nonverbal diagnosis. I will never forget the joy on all of our faces the day when Patrick, after years of speech therapy, finally blew out his birthday candles for the first time. I know that is something I take for granted. It seems that so many of the struggles we have with Patrick, so much of his suffering, would be gone if he could only speak and tell us what he needs or how he feels. Hardly a day goes by when Patrick doesn't come to us at least once, with big tears rolling down his face, trying to communicate something to us that we just can't understand. None of the communication aids has worked very well for him. It seems when he really needed something, he would be too upset to point to a communication board or use signs. Over the years, Patrick has learned to use a few words and signs (potty, more, done, no) when he really needs to, but even those are hard to understand. We are elated when we hear one new word. I have been able to understand from Patrick's silence what a truly awesome gift speech is.

God has used Patrick to speak volumes without a word leaving his lips. One of my aunts, Sister Maria Tasto, a Benedictine sister from Ferdinand, Indiana, was very sick with cancer, and just before undergoing surgery, while sitting on the couch with Patrick, she felt him put his hand on her leg. She was worried about the surgery, but when he looked at her, she said it was as if he were saying, "Everything will be all right, Sister." A certain peace came over her, and although in the months that followed she almost died, she now has had a miraculous, almost complete recovery. Many times Patrick will hold my face in his hands and gaze into my eyes. The moment is brief, but I can tell there is so much he wants to say. Patrick holds so much inside, but he cannot express it like most others. Until God gives him the gift of speech, we will have to rely upon the warmth of his eyes or a gentle touch.

To this day, I still find little traces of pink nail polish in the bathroom. They are little reminders of my prayers for control of my tongue. But the greatest reminder of all is a little child who has been so beautifully fashioned by God to love Him and serve Him. That's my Patrick.

O LORD, our Lord, how majestic is thy name in all the earth!
Thou whose glory above the heavens is chanted by
the mouth of babes and infants . . .

—Psalm 8:1-2

CHAPTER NINETEEN

Dancing through the Night

October 8, 2000

My dear Patrick,

You are no longer here to keep me awake at night. Even Emily is sleeping through the night now, at least most of the time. And yet, here I am, awake, wishing you were here with me. Each time I leave you, I carry with me all the pain and the hurt I see you suffer. You did not want to let go of my hand when we left Silvercrest today, and I did not want to let go of yours.

As usual, it was a beautiful day we spent together at the zoo. I have always loved the zoo, especially the monkeys. I can remember being a little girl standing in the kitchen with my mother, begging her to let me have a baby monkey of my own. She knew better. Today I got to hold your hand while we stood together watching the little monkeys jump around and play.

My happiness came not from the monkeys, but from seeing you smile. With each new animal, your brothers and sisters stood close to you to see the way your face lights up when you see something you like. You always seem to enjoy the animals in the water the most. I know you would love to climb in with the sea lions or seals. You make us laugh each time you squeal with delight when one swims by. We all want so much to share in your happiness and shelter you from pain.

The best way we know of to help you is to pray for you, Patrick, and we do. We pray for you along with many people all over the world. I think that is why I'm awake right now, not to cry, but to pray for your comfort and happiness during this seemingly endless confusion in your life. Sleep well. God bless you, my little one.

I love you,
Mommy

*For you have need of endurance, so that you may
do the will of God and receive what is promised.*

—*Hebrews 10:36*

*E*xhausted, I slipped between the sheets. It felt so good to close my eyes in the silence of the night and know that it would be another three or four hours until the baby, Emily, awoke again to nurse. Even though I loved waking to nurse her, knowing that I could comfort and soothe whatever it was that was upsetting her, I was very tired. All I could think of was that I needed sleep. God, along with Mark and each of my children, knows how irritable I can be when I don't get enough sleep.

Just then it happened—one of the sounds that I dread most in the night. Not the sounds of bombs exploding over the heads of my sleeping children, although that is a real fear for many mothers. Not the sounds of some intruder. Not even the sounds of strange animals outside my window. No, my dreaded sound came in the form of "Chim chiminey, chim chiminey, chim chim cher-ee! A sweep is as lucky, as lucky can be. Chim chiminey, chim chiminey, chim chim cher-oo! Good luck will rub off when I shake 'ands with you."

The song swept me quickly from my bed. I flew into the living room as swiftly as my feet could carry me. My eyes beheld Patrick laughing and jumping from one couch to the other while he did his best impersonation of a chimney sweep. The volume was blaring, and I knew that at any moment I could have not one child awake, but nine.

I decreased the volume considerably and sank down on the couch and began to pray. "O Lord, I can't do this. I'm so tired." Then I closed my eyes and listened. The words that came to my heart were not "You'll make it. He'll be asleep soon, and you can go back to bed." Those were the words I was hoping for. What I heard caught me completely off guard. The Lord asked,

"Will you go into the lions' den for me?" My immediate answer was yes. I would not hesitate.

Ever since I was a child, I had read about the early martyrs of the Church. Their faith and courage in the face of such suffering touched me deeply, at times to the point of tears. I would pray, "Lord, give me the kind of faith that would allow me to accept that kind of suffering for you." As I sat there that night watching Patrick flying around the room, hopping from one piece of furniture to the next in an almost frantic state, I took a deep breath. Then, I completed my answer to the Lord, "Yes, I will go into the lions' den for you, but please, not the monkey cage." At that moment the magnitude of the lions' den hit me hard. I realized that if I did not have the endurance to suffer what God was asking of me that night, then I surely didn't have what it would take to enter a den of wild, starving animals. The lions' den was at the end of the race, and I was in the early stages of training. God's grace opened my heart that night to see that I should embrace every opportunity to strengthen my muscles and increase my endurance.

When I looked at Patrick again, I thought to myself, "What is the difference between waking to care for him and waking for little Emily? Something was bothering him, and he woke up." "I couldn't comfort him as I can comfort Emily," I reflected, "but I could be there while he watched his movie, a movie that brought him such great joy and somehow soothed some of the pain or frustration that he was feeling." Patrick then came to me and curled up on my lap. His bright eyes left the television and gazed into mine with all the sweetness of a little baby. He was ready to calm down, to rest in my arms, to be comforted by his mommy, even if it was for only a brief moment.

I came to see that night that it would take many more nights in the monkey cage before I would ever be ready for the lions' den. God would not give up on me. I knew He would not send me to the lions' den without all the grace that it would take to endure until the end. And as surely as the sun would be there, rising at the start of a new day, so, too, would His grace be there, helping me make it through each day, minute by minute. For now, I just needed to curl up on the couch with my little monkey and be willing to watch *Mary Poppins* at least one more time.

And the streets of the city shall be full of
boys and girls playing in its streets.

—*Zechariah 8:5*

CHAPTER TWENTY

Raising Saints

November 1, 2000

My dear Patrick,

Today is one of your special days. It's All Saints' Day. Last night, we had saint costumes from one end of the house to the other, and there among them all was your dragon costume. It was hard to hold back the tears. This will be the first year in many that you are not running through the house to every mirror to see yourself in the dragon costume. Last night, I sat at the sewing machine, mending all the little tears you've made in the costume over the years. Brendan will be the dragon this year because Michael wants to be Saint George, the dragon slayer. It was hard to hold the costume in my hands and not hold you. Oh, Patrick, my arms ache to hold you.

We went to an All Saints' party today. One of the little boys was dressed as Saint Patrick. You are named after him. He did so much to teach people about Christ and His love. The people were living in darkness. I thought to myself, "I know another Saint Patrick, a very special little saint, a masterpiece of God." Patrick, you have the body of an athlete, and yet you may never play sports. You have a love for music, and you may never play an instrument. You can't even say the beautiful name of Jesus. Yet daily you teach others about Christ and His love.

Tonight, we are going to watch a movie on the life of Saint Patrick. As a young boy, Saint Patrick was taken from his parents and sold into slavery in Ireland. I'm sure his mother wondered many of the same things I do. "Is my Patrick okay? Is he cold or hungry?" It's so hard not to know. She didn't even know if he was alive. It's beautiful that God used Saint Patrick's absence from home to plant in his heart the seeds of love for the people he would one day baptize. God is using you, too, through all the tears. His plan is amazing—of that we can be sure. God bless you, my little one.

I love you,
Mommy

———◆◆◆———

Therefore, since we are surrounded
by so great a cloud of witnesses,
let us also lay aside every weight, and sin
which clings so closely,
and let us run with perseverance
the race that is set before us.

—Hebrews 12:1

"I always thought I would have time to write. My dream was to stay home and take care of my children and write children's books," my friend said. She sighed and went on, "The years keep going by, and I haven't written a single book. Some days I'm lucky just to get the dishes done—and the laundry, well, I don't know if I'll ever catch up on that." I could see in her eyes that she was feeling overwhelmed, and her words that followed told me why. "If I could only get done all that I need to around the house, then I would have time to write, but it just seems to be getting worse, not better."

My friend loved being a mother. No one could question that. What I did wonder was if she understood the magnitude of what she was doing. I asked her why she felt she should be writing. She told me, "I feel I should be doing something to use my degree and to develop this talent God gave me." I shared with her my story of how God showed me it was time to stop working at the hospital as a nurse. He had greater plans for me.

I loved being a nurse. Cardiac nursing was my favorite. The more I learned about the heart, the more I was in awe of God's creation, and this whole area of nursing fascinated me. The part I liked most, however, was taking care of the patients, especially the elderly. In many ways it was so much like taking care of my children. They needed to be held, fed, cleaned, and medicated, but most of all, they needed love. I told myself this was where I could best use the talents God gave me, not to mention the extra income to help with our growing family. I only worked part-time, in the evenings or on weekends. Mark was always home, so it did not seem to be a big deal, except that I could hear in my heart God telling me to stay home.

Little by little, I began to see how even those few nights a week were stressful for my family. It meant that Mark was left to do the dishes, to give baths, and to get the children into bed. Patrick was five at the time and was becoming increasingly difficult. Mark did a wonderful job, but it was stressful for him, in part because it left no time for him to grade the many papers he brought home each night.

On the days after I worked at the hospital, we were both tired. It usually took an entire day for me to recover. It was difficult to get things done around the house because I was so tired and because my patience with the children was very short. I knew in my heart I was supposed to stop working, but it just didn't make sense. I loved what I was doing. I was good at it, and we needed the money. I would not let go of nursing; I was holding on so tightly. God knew that I would not let go, and so He showed me just what He wanted me to hold on to.

I explained to my friend that it was not in church or while gazing up at the stars that He showed me that it was time to stop working. No, I was at a stoplight at an extremely busy intersection in the midst of the city. There I sat in my big white van with Patrick buckled in the seat beside me and four very noisy children behind me. I was going through a mental checklist of all I needed to get done that day. Feeling more than a little overwhelmed, I turned around to be sure everyone was okay. Suddenly, I could not hear the children. Their mouths were moving, but I was fixed on their faces. I could hear from inside my heart, "These are the children, the little souls, I need you to get ready for heaven. For this I have prepared you." At that moment my eyes were opened to the tremendous responsibility and vocation of motherhood. Not only would Patrick need a great deal of care, but all of my little ones, including Michael, the one I carried inside me, would need the best I had to give.

My immediate reaction under the weight of such a difficult task was one of fear, but God quickly poured peace into my soul. It was a peace of knowing that it would be in the everyday, little things—the laundry, the diaper changes, the hugs, the words of kindness, the prayers—that these little souls would be formed. When the stoplight changed, I drove on, but I continued to glance over at Patrick. I thought of the many mothers, over hundreds of years, who had prepared their children to live for Christ and one day be with Him in heaven. Somehow they did so in the quiet of their homes under the mask of daily housework. They passed on their faith and taught their children about the unconditional love of God. They were raising saints.

I did not know it at the time, but now I am sure that the seeds were being planted for Mark and me to homeschool our children. As my knowledge of the importance of our children's faith formation has grown, my desire to be with them every step of the way has increased. Through years of prayer and discernment, we eventually felt God was calling us to do just that. God provided us with the perfect opportunity to begin our home school when we moved to Loogootee. It was a chance to begin anew. It has been an incredible experience that I believe has brought Mark and me closer to our children than we could have ever imagined.

I went on to explain to my friend that I no longer found working at the hospital very exciting. It all seemed rather dull. In fact, even being a brain surgeon or a rocket scientist sounds rather boring compared to preparing souls for heaven. I said, "A brain surgeon holds in his hands the tools to change the brain. Mothers are the instruments God uses to transform the minds of children, to draw them closer to Him. As for a rocket scientist, his job is to find a way for the rocket ship to break through the pull of gravity and leave the earth's atmosphere. Mothers are the rockets God uses to carry children toward heaven, away from the pull of this world."

As I said good-bye to my friend, the door opened, and there was Patrick. He had tears streaming down his face. He wanted me to hold him, and as I did, I thought of how many times I've heard other mothers say, "I don't know how you do it with Patrick. I know I couldn't." "No," I thought, "they could not do what I am doing, and I could not do what God is calling them to do. I am the only one called to run this particular course." God molded and fashioned me; then He set the course before me. With the promise that He would give me everything I needed, He asked me to run. How could I say no? As I held Patrick, I thanked God that I would be spending my days doing laundry, scrubbing toilets, baking cookies, reading stories, wiping noses, giving kisses, and pushing swings. I'll spend my days here in my home, raising saints.

See what love the Father has given us, that we should be called children of God; and so we are. The reason why the world does not know us is that it did not know him.

—1 John 3:1

CHAPTER TWENTY-ONE

From the Hand of God

November 17, 2000

My dear Patrick,

Tomorrow, Grandma, Grandpa, and Laura will be at Silvercrest to bring you home for Thanksgiving. As always, Grandpa wants to be there early to pick you up. They can hardly wait to see you. Like the rest of us, they have missed you very much. They offered to help out because Daddy is at a teachers' conference at the University of Notre Dame.

Once again my heart is filled with both joy at your coming home and sadness that in a short time you will have to return to school. I look forward to the day we do not have to take you back, the day you can come home to stay. The hurt, confused look on your face when we take you back is almost more than I can bear. Patrick, I know we are to be thankful for all the Lord has given us, even this year when you are away from home, but it is so hard.

God has always given us so much to be thankful for. Today, Daddy brought all the winter coats in from storage. When I opened the first tub, there was one of your old winter coats. As I stood there holding it, my eyes filled with tears, remembering all the times I saw you wear it. I remembered the many hours you spent playing outside in that coat. You have always loved chewing on clothing, as I could clearly see. The sleeves and collar were covered in holes, and the zipper was beyond repair. Like most of your clothes and coats, I knew I would not be able to pass it on to your brothers, but that's okay. We always have enough coats, and even some to give away. God will always take care of us, and He will get us through the pain and hurt. We can rest in His care. I can hardly wait to see you tomorrow. I love you so much. God bless you, my little one.

I love you,
Mommy

*Therefore I tell you, do not be anxious about your life, what
you shall eat, nor about your body, what you shall put on.*

—*Luke 12:22*

*T*he children ran to the front door as a truck pulled up
the driveway. The excitement of someone coming to
visit always makes them eager to see who it is. On this
particular day, it was a friend, Doctor Nonte, with his wife and
two sons. Doctor Nonte had mentioned earlier to Mark that
they had some boxes of their daughter Emily's clothing they
wanted to give us.

We have always tried to accept happily what God offers us
through others, and then pass on what we don't need. As a rule,
I never lend anything out. I only give it away. I never want
another mother to have to worry about returning things to me
and taking good care of them. God always sends them back
when I need them, in a new form, and in better condition than
when they left.

As the truck was unloaded, my dining room table began to
disappear under what seemed like an endless flow of boxes
filled with beautiful coats, shirts, pants, dresses, and shoes. The
only things we needed that weren't in the boxes were jeans and
dress shoes for Michael. Michael is very hard on his jeans, and
the only ones he had were ready for the trash.

By the time the truck was empty, the boxes were stacked
halfway to the ceiling. I knew if I left it up to my children, the
clothes would be spread from one end of the house to the
other. Patrick loves trying on clothes. No matter what the size,
he makes them fit. Once he even found Sean's newborn Santa
suit, and somehow slipped his arms through the sleeves and
proceeded to bounce around the house very happy with himself. Quickly, I began to sort the wonderful contents of the
boxes, determined to find a home for each item. It was only a
few hours till dinner, and we needed the table. I had to act fast.

As the clothes slipped through my fingers and into piles according to everyone's needs, I thought of a concern people had expressed to us when we were trying to decide if God wanted us to move to this small town. They were worried that the people of Loogootee wouldn't be as helpful or as generous as the people of Carmel had been. It warmed my heart to know that what they said could not have been further from the truth.

The Body of Christ knows no boundaries. Yes, friends in Carmel had indeed gone out of their way to help us not only with Patrick, but also in many ways with our other children. Their concerns did not make sense to me because three of the most giving and generous people I knew in Carmel were from the area where we now live. Mark and two of our neighbors, Mike and Marilyn Bullock, all grew up in this part of southern Indiana. I knew there had to be more people like them, and I was right.

Before we even moved, people began to offer to help us in any way they could, and this assistance has not stopped since. I can't count the number of times people have offered to lend a hand. It has been incredible. There are meals, clothes, help with watching Patrick, anonymous cards with money slipped in—the list goes on and on. Yet everyone gives as if it were no big deal. We have been showered with more help than we could have ever imagined.

As I finished sorting the clothes, I looked at all the piles to be passed on to friends and others in need. God was providing not only for my family, but also for many others. There was even a stack of beautiful clothes for the little girl across the street whose house had burnt to the ground, and yet another for a home for unwed mothers.

I thought about the extent to which caring for Patrick had left us dependent on others. I wondered, "If it weren't for Patrick's autism, would we need so much help?" Then I heard the gentle voice of my heavenly Father speaking to me about how we are all in need of Him. He let me know that I am not dependent on others, only on Him, and I'm no more dependent on Him than anyone else is. He helped me to see that the air we breathe comes from Him, and the heart only beats at His command. Even all the clothes before me came first from His hand.

By the time we sat down for dinner, the table had been cleared, all the clothes had been put in closets and drawers, and the boxes to be given away had been carried to the van. As we finished thanking God for the meal and all He has blessed us with, I looked around the table at my little girls, who were already wearing some of their new clothes. They were all smiles. It has never once bothered any of my children that someone else wore the clothes first. To them, even clothes that have been in storage for a season are new when we take them out again.

A short while later, a friend called to ask if she could stop by with some clothes for Michael. She said, "It's not much, but there are several pairs of jeans, shirts, and dress shoes." I had just recognized the need, and God was there to provide. What else could I do? I said, "Yes!"—not only to her, but also to God. In my heart, I knew that no matter what I do, no matter how much I have—with or without an autistic child—I am, like everyone else, completely dependent on Him for everything.

He is ever giving liberally and lending,
and his children become a blessing.

—Psalm 37:26

CHAPTER TWENTY-TWO

Hope without Healing

December 8, 2000

My dear Patrick,

You are finally coming home. Having you away from us has been harder than I could have ever imagined. I don't know that the tears will ever stop coming, or that my arms will ever stop aching to hold you, but knowing you will be home for Christmas has been a great comfort. Patrick, you are such a part of our Christmas joy. It's not the tree, the presents, or the food, that makes Christmas wonderful. They are only expressions of our joy. Nor is "being together as a family" the most important part of Christmas; Christ is the center of Christmas.

I will never forget Christmas 1991, which occurred just after we found out you are autistic. It was what I call the best of all Christmases and the worst of all Christmases. It was the worst from a worldly point of view, because your Grandfather Gibbons, who loved you very much, had died of pancreatic cancer a few months before. You were so dear to him. I have many happy memories of him following you around the yard or pushing you on the swing. It was hard to think of Christmas without Grandpa. Just a month before Grandpa died, his mother, your great grandma, died. She was ready to go to heaven, and Grandpa's illness was very hard on her. Someone who had been very dear to us, Maria, also died. Maria was in the youth group that Daddy and I volunteered for at church. She was just starting her freshman year of college when she was killed in a car accident. My heart ached for her family and friends, who would be missing her so much. Everyone who knew Maria knew that the source of her joy was her love for Christ. She openly shared her faith with everyone.

There were many other things that could have been causes for great stress that Christmas. You and all your brothers and sisters had the stomach flu. I tried to prepare a beautiful Christmas dinner, but Daddy and I were the only ones who could eat. The washer and dryer ran night and day. I was about to give birth to Megan, and each step I took caused great pain. Even opening the few gifts we could afford was difficult. Everyone just wanted to go back to bed. So much of what many believe makes for a beautiful Christmas was taken from me that year, and yet my joy was greater than ever before.

Indeed, it was the best of all Christmases. Every time I looked at you, all I could think of was that you will be perfect in heaven because of Christmas Day. And not only you, but also Maria, Grandpa, and Great Grandma will be able to live forever in heaven because God gave us His Son. The loss of loved ones and the diagnosis of your autism, something for which there is no cure, only made me look more closely at what Christmas is truly about. Nothing in this world could take away the comfort and joy that came to me that Christmas.

We will be there soon to bring you home, so that you can fill our house with your noise, your messes, your tears, and your laughter. You will be able to fill our home with the true joy of Christmas. We miss you so much. God bless you, my little one.

I love you,
Mommy

For he has made known to us in all wisdom and insight the mystery of his will, according to his purpose which he set forth in Christ as a plan for the fulness of time, to unite all things in him, things in heaven and things on earth.

—Ephesians 1:9-10

My little five-year-old son, Michael, said one morning, "I want an egg sandwich," to which I replied, "No, you don't." "Yes, I do. I'm so hungry," he moaned. "Michael, I'm sure you don't want an egg sandwich, and you need to smile and be happy about it," I said. We went back and forth like this for five minutes or so before I finally said, "Michael, you need to work with me here. You will be very sad if I make you an egg sandwich, so please be happy and say you don't want one." Eventually, with great hesitation, Michael let those few words pass his lips: "I don't want an egg sandwich." When he looked at me with his big, pleading eyes, I could see his heart was not in his words. "Michael, you've almost got it, but now I want you to smile about it. I want to see teeth." After a few little sighs and questioning looks, with a big grin on his face, he said, "I don't want an egg sandwich." Quickly, I said, "Good, because if you wanted an egg sandwich, I would have made it for you, and then I wouldn't have enough eggs to make the chocolate chip cookies I'm planning to bake for you." His grin turned into a huge smile.

As he hugged me, I thought about how relatively short a time it took to convince a hungry five year old that he didn't want what he was hungry for and actually to be happy about it. "How long will it take God to get through to me?" I wondered. "How long will it take for me to know in my heart that what I'm longing for, what I want for Patrick, needs to be only what God wants for Patrick?" I think I want Patrick living at home, but he's not home. I want him calm, but he's far from calm. I want him to able to go to Mass with us, but the noise in the church hurts his ears. At any given moment, he jumps up and lets out a high-pitched shriek. I want Patrick to be able to talk, but he can't. I want him to be comfortable, but he's often in pain.

These are not bad things for a mother to want for her little boy. It is just that at this time, it is not what is best for Patrick and our family. God wants so much more for Patrick than my limited, little human heart can comprehend. What I desire for Patrick cannot even come close to what God desires for him. Slowly, little by little, God is whispering to my heart, "Work with me here." And, as Michael had resolved to say, "I don't want an egg sandwich," I have finally resolved to want only what God wants for Patrick. I still have a long way to go, however, until I am happy about accepting God's will for Patrick and actually being glad that I'm not getting what I want. Long ago, we placed Patrick in God's hands. Our constant prayer is "Thy will be done," asking Him to watch over and care for our little one. I know He will never let go.

When God gave Patrick to us, He gave us the great privilege of loving and caring for him. Part of that is looking for a cure and providing the best treatment we can. He did not ask us to find a cure, only to look for one. We have been all over the country on this quest. In California, Patrick saw a doctor who is doing wonderful research on the connection between autistic behavior and the immune system. Many children and adults have been greatly helped by his work. With Patrick, we saw very little change. We took him to Milwaukee to see a doctor who has had great success with the use of antifungal medication and a change in diet. We saw no change. I spent days on the phone trying to find a doctor who would give Patrick secretin injections. Patrick's stomach pain seemed to improve after the injections, but there was no change in his autistic behavior.

There is a constant flow of research on autism that can keep a parent flying all over the country, only to have one specialist say one thing, and then have the next say the exact opposite. Each and every step of the way, prayer has guided us, leading us on the path God has chosen for us.

Even when I see Patrick cry, I know that he is in the loving hands of his Father. When I see the most beautiful rays of sunlight streaming through the clouds, I know that without the clouds, my human eyes would never be able to see such a magnificent display of God's beauty—a foretaste of heaven.

Children are a beautiful stairway to heaven. Slowly, day after day, hour after hour, minute after minute, they work with

God to help us grow in virtue and to scrape away all the filth that covers us because of our sins. God is trying to make us saints and is using precious little children to help Him. Knowing my weakness, God in His infinite wisdom gave me not a stairway but an escalator to heaven.

While it may seem long, our life on earth is so short. It comes and goes in a heartbeat. Someday very soon, Patrick will be healed. He will no longer suffer in frustration and pain. This world may not see it, but we know that when he joins the angels and the saints for all eternity, he will be healed. He will be perfect. Forever he will shine with the glory of God for all to see. For now, while I cannot hold him in my arms, I will hold my little Patrick in my heart and thank God for the privilege of being his mother and having been in the presence of such a precious treasure.

Lo! I tell you a mystery. We shall not all sleep, but we shall all be changed, in a moment, in the twinkling of an eye, at the last trumpet. For the trumpet will sound, and the dead will be raised imperishable, and we shall be changed.

—*1 Corinthians 15:51-52*

Afterword

Thank You, Lord, for the dirty walls smudged with sticky fingerprints and marked with crayons. The walls would be spotless if it weren't for the chubby little fingers, learning to reach for You, that gently trace my face with love. Lord, thank You for my little ones.

Thank You, Lord, for the stack of dirty dishes and the kitchen counter covered with traces of peanut butter and jelly. They would be clean if it weren't for the beautiful little mouths that can't seem to kiss me enough. Lord, thank You for my little ones.

Thank You, Lord, for the piles of laundry stained in grape juice, grass, and mashed banana. There would be little to wash if it weren't for the precious little bodies that I get to hold next to mine. Lord, thank You for my little ones.

Thank You, Lord, for the lost shoes, hidden in the mess of books, toys, and treasures under the bed. They would not need to be found if it weren't for the soft little feet I've held in my hands and tickled time and again. Lord, thank You for my little ones.

Thank You, Lord, for the tracks of footprints throughout the house. My carpet would be spotless if it weren't for the strong, little legs that run quickly to greet me when I walk through the door. Lord, thank You for my little ones.

Thank You, Lord, for each tipped glass of milk that makes a mess on the table and floor. There would be no spills if it weren't for the tender arms that wrap around my neck in hugs that never want to end. Lord, thank You for my little ones.

Thank You, Lord, for the unmade beds and the blankets thrown here and there. They would be neatly made if it weren't for the sleepy little eyes that light up when they see me in the morning. Lord, thank You for my little ones.

Thank You, Lord, for all the disobedience and misbehavior even after the hundredth time I've given directions. My guidance would not be needed if it weren't for the cute little ears that have listened for the comfort of my voice since the day they were formed. Lord, thank You for my little ones.

Thank You, Lord, for the endless noise, the crying, whining, and screaming at play. There would be silence if it weren't for the sweet little voices that whisper in my ear, "Mommy, I love you." Lord, thank You for my little ones.

Thank You, Lord, for the suffering, the pain, and the sorrow. There would be no need for Band-Aids, or tissue to wipe away tears, if it weren't for the souls You've placed in my care for today. A time may come when You must take them away, and my lips won't move, but my heart will say, "Lord, thank You for my little ones."

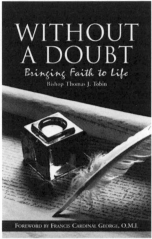